Just A Stage

*All the world's a stage,
but when will they grow out of this one?*

Humorous stories on each stage of children's lives,
with tips to help you
laugh, love and live through them

Jan Butsch

Jan Butsch

Schroder Media, LLC
www.schrodermedia.com
Atlanta, Georgia

ISBN: 0-9762288-0-7

Published by Schroder Media, LLC
Atlanta, GA.
www.schrodermedia.com

Library of Congress Cataloging-in-Publication
    Data
Butsch, Janice Richey
Just A Stage/Jan Butsch
First Edition

LCCN: 2004097994

This book is dedicated to my children,
Catherine and Christopher.

In addition to inspiration for the
stories in this book,
you bring me joy, love and laughter every day.

All my love, forever.

Mom

Contents

Three: School Days

Four: Vacations and Celebrations

Introduction

"Humor is emotional chaos remembered in tranquility."
– *James Thurber*

I love this quote and thought it described my writing perfectly. And then I thought, what tranquility? James Thurber was not a mother. I know because I looked it up. So I can agree that emotional chaos fuels my humor, but I wouldn't have written a word all these years if I had been waiting for that tranquility thing to kick in.

I was going to call this book "All the World's a Stage, But When Are They Going To Grow Out Of This One?" But then I remembered my rapidly declining attention span, which I figure I share with other parents, and I didn't want you to get bored before you even finished the title. So here it is: Just a Stage.

If you buy this book, I would like for you to get two things out of it. 1) Support for the exhausting, exhilarating, incomparable task of parenting and 2) Some good laughs to make your day go just a little bit better.

I was at a party many years ago when two women sat down near me. "So, do you sterilize your nipples in boiling water?" one asked the other.

After cringing with the painful implications that such an endeavor would cause and wondering if I missed something revolutionary in the latest issue of

Cosmopolitan, I realized that these were two new mothers discussing baby bottles.

Now, after having children of my own, I understand that in addition to offering each other feeding tips they were giving each other something that all parents need - support.

This is the one thing you can't find in the Right Start catalog, amidst the diaper pails that compact and gently scent the diaper, or the wipe warmers and drool catchers. But it's one thing I think all parents need, from the first days of babyhood through adolescence.

Becoming a parent has no job training. It's not like being in school or having outside employment where there is a system of grades or rewards and you have an idea of how you're doing. After a difficult moment with a tantrum-throwing two-year-old, or a heated exchange with an adolescent, there is no one to tell you that you handled it well or you did the right thing. You need to rely on outside support.

Support can come in many forms. I found it once in an article about TV ratings. The article discussed audiences for all-night programming and mentioned nursing mothers. At the time, I was nursing my first child, Catherine, and was dragging myself bleary-eyed and bedraggled from bed several times a night to slump semi-comatose while she nursed. Sometimes I would turn on the TV.

A male friend of mine suggested I use the time to watch the news shows. I laughed and told him that in my present sleep-deprived condition, following the plot line of "Laverne and Shirley" would be a stretch. If Laverne didn't wear those sweaters with the big "L" on them, I would not even be able to keep the characters straight.

Reading the article didn't change anything. Catherine still wanted to nurse just as much, but the next night, when I got up at 2 a.m., I felt better. The article let me know I wasn't the only one.

I used to teach parenting classes and lead seminars

on communication skills to help parents improve their relationships with their children. An additional benefit parents receive in taking such a course is mutual support. So when a mother comes to class and says, "I stirred my daughter's yogurt and she didn't want me to and then I cut her sandwich the wrong way and she cried and cried. Am I a bad mother?" we can tell her absolutely not. You are the mother of a two-year-old.

We don't have any baby bottles or diapers in our house any longer, but my need for support from other parents hasn't changed. Each phase of childhood brings its own challenges. I hope to provide some support to parents in this book.

So remember, when you are having one of those days - when the baby throws up again on your new sweater, or your four-year-old screams that he hates you while you are in the grocery store because you won't buy the double-frosted pop tarts with sprinkles, or your 10-year-old informs you at 10:00 at night that tomorrow is Biography Day and she needs a costume to be Madame Curie, or your teenager wants to borrow the car for the first time - seek support from your fellow parents. You are not alone.

Here are a few more James Thurber quotes I love.

"Laughter need not be cut out of anything, since it improves everything."

"Love is what you've been through with somebody."

I hope you read this book and enjoy it. And share it with someone you love.

●

Jan Butsch
Atlanta, Georgia

One

A Child is Born

Myth Conceptions

Things I thought I knew about pregnancy
but was way wrong

You can read a lot about pregnancy these days and have a pretty good idea of what to expect during this joyous yet confusing phase of a woman's life. But books can't cover everything, so on occasion, I found myself filling in the missing information for myself.

Here are a few of my own myths from pregnancy and early days of motherhood.

You can eat whatever you want. After reading about all the extra calories you need each day while you're pregnant, I immediately and gleefully abandoned the life-long chore of watching my waistline. Besides, I couldn't wait to start wearing maternity clothes, and if that daily chocolate chip cookie habit sped the process along, so much the better!

Ever since I was in third grade, when it became apparent that my baby fat had annoyingly followed me into childhood, I had struggled with my weight. I finally told my mother to stop calling it "pleasingly plump." I didn't know anyone who was at all pleased about it, except maybe the boys at school who always picked me as the first girl on the softball team because my weight had a lot of heft behind it, but I knew I sure wasn't happy about it. I won't say I was fat, but I did take up more than my fair share of gravity. It took me until I was 17 to shed the extra pounds, and each of them fought back pretty hard.

So it was with great delight that about five months into my pregnancy I discovered I had not gained a pound since my last weigh-in three weeks before. What better way to celebrate than to add a large slice of chocolate cheesecake to the daily cookie?

Three weeks later I heaved myself onto the scales. I had gained eight pounds in three weeks. Enough said. As one doctor said to a friend of mine, "We're just trying to make a baby here."

You can prepare your nipples for nursing. The books said to toughen up your nipples at the end of your pregnancy by rubbing them with a rough washcloth. So I'd stand in the shower, all 150 plus pounds of me, roughing up my nipples. (If you find anything at all attractive in this image, please seek help immediately. There is something seriously wrong with you.) For those of you who haven't experienced such a joy, I will report that this is one of those times that you are actually embarrassed in front of yourself. As to its effectiveness, that would be questionable. Babies latch on with all the sucking power of a Hoover vacuum when they are hungry, and I'm not sure of anything that can prepare you for that.

I would love having big breasts while nursing. I did

not. All those big-breasted women carry those things around like they are sacs of gold, and act like they've got such an advantage. Maybe they do in a lot of ways. But it takes a lot of energy to haul those balloon-like obstacles around, and they kind of got in the way. I'd reach across the table for the mashed potatoes, but instead of reaching straight, I had to go around. My blouses wouldn't button right.

The worst was if I attended an event with a nametag, I sometimes had a suspicion the men weren't just checking out the spelling of my last name. Once I said to one who was being particularly obvious, "I bet you're admiring my tough nipples, aren't you?" As he beat a hasty retreat, no doubt to find a more cordial big-breasted woman, I yelled after him, "If you're heading to the dessert table I could use another chocolate-chip cookie!"

Pregnant women are moody and hormonal. Just because I once sobbed riding the stationary bike while watching the latex-wearing young girls in aerobics class jump up and down and once had a screaming fit because a potato exploded in the toaster oven, doesn't mean ... well, okay. So this one is kinda true.

I looked good in my maternity bathing suit. That bathing suit, along with the horizontally striped dresses I wore, belongs in my "What Was I Thinking?" Hall of Fame, even surpassing the lace-up hip-huggers I wore in the '70s. The pink-and-white striped suit covered my ever-expanding thighs, so I thought all was well. The photos suggest otherwise: I looked like a carousel with feet. We were able to recycle it, however. We used the top as a tarp for our house when we took the roof off of our kitchen for a renovation.

Here's one final myth of pregnancy. This one has been around for a while and I don't know what the latest consensus is, but it has been said that *drinking beer helps moms produce milk*. I've never seen a cow drink beer so I'm a little dubious on this one. I suspect a desperate mom made this one up to get her husband off her back. But I do know after giving up alcohol for nine months, and dealing with the sleep-deprived, wild and wacky days of early motherhood, a cold Killian's Red produced a happier mom.

✐ Pregnancy Tip
It is best not to make plans for renovating your house, writing a book, or starting a new business during maternity leave. Depending on the type of baby you have, a more realistic goal may be to take a shower and eat lunch, all in the same day.

☺ Web Wit
When one woman was six months pregnant with her third child, her three-year-old came into the room when she was just getting ready to get into the shower.

She said, "Mommy, you are getting fat!" Mom replied, "Yes, honey, remember Mommy has a baby growing in her tummy."

"I know," she replied, "but what's growing in your butt?"

A State of Bliss

Things I'm glad I didn't know before giving birth

They say ignorance is bliss. I believe this saying applies to a lot of things. I am totally blissful that I don't know the actual ingredients of a hot dog or how many dust mites are in my mattress. It thrills me that I have no clue when Elvis' birthday is, how many stomachs a llama has, or the best way to clean a trout. There is a wonderful freedom in declaring, "I don't know and I don't care."

There are definitely things about becoming a mom I am glad I didn't know before I joined the ranks of the progeny enhanced.

I am very glad I didn't know my son would weigh 9 pounds 8 ounces when he was born, or that he would have a Charlie Brown melon head. (Sorry, Christopher, it's true. But you've grown into it nicely.) When asked what kind of baby she wanted, one woman I know answered, "One with a small head." I wasn't so lucky.

No one ever told me I was going to have a big baby, and for this lack of knowledge I am truly grateful. What possible good would it have done me if the doctor had said at the end of my pregnancy, "Whoa! Sign up for heavy drugs how because you're going to have a heck of a time getting that one out!" Then all those sleepless nights I had because I was so uncomfortable in my largeness, I would have just sat/laid there, feeling even sorrier for myself and becoming increasingly depressed at the thought of getting what was in *there*, out *here*. Instead, I just sat there thinking about my craving for Cherry Garcia ice cream, but not having any because, 1) we didn't have any in the house, and 2) the amount of effort it required to actually get out of bed even if we did. So then I could still be sleepless, but feel like a martyr about the whole thing at the same time.

I could have guessed I'd have a big baby. Unlike some of my friends that just looked like they'd had a big dinner when they were nine months pregnant, I was of a more bulbous nature. I couldn't see my feet after about month seven and had to have the UPS man tie my shoes on more than one occasion.

It must have been hormonally induced insanity that forced me to buy knit dresses at Rich's with horizontal stripes. Anyone who reads "Vogue" or the Fashion Police section of Us magazine, my personal favorite, or has done a little people watching at Six Flags knows horizontal stripes make you appear wider. When I look back on pictures of myself, I realize I looked like a gigantic mobile blue and white beach umbrella. The joke, "When God said 'Let there be light' he asked you to move," certainly applied to me.

It became really embarrassing when we were standing on the hill of St. Philip's Cathedral on the 4th of July watching the annual Peachtree Road Race and a mother carefully spread out a blanket and placed her three children in my shadow. When her husband asked me how long I would be there and then strategically placed the cooler next to me as well, I almost said something.

I've heard it said that childbirth is like trying to squeeze a St. Bernard through a cat door. In my case it was more like a baby hippo.

I'm also glad I didn't know that I wouldn't like shopping for myself any more. It happened time and time again. I'd go shopping for some clothes that were non-maternity and had been manufactured sometime within the current presidential term. My body was still not recognizable as my own – my weight had redistributed in places that were pleasing (my chest) and not so pleasing (my thighs.) I read somewhere that nursing mothers maintain fat on their thighs so they can continue to feed their babies should a famine occur. I could rest quite comfortably at night knowing that should our food supply be completely cut off overnight, I could quite easily nourish my children until they were through grade school and could forage for berries in the woods on their own.

So none of my clothes fit right. At the mall I'd think about what I'd need to wear to an upcoming party and which stores I'd visit. Hours later I'd head home with a full trunk of, you guessed it, clothes for the baby. The thing about baby clothes is that they are all so adorable and would look especially adorable on my baby. I couldn't risk another baby wearing my baby's outfit so I bought them all.

At the party I would make sure my conversation was especially scintillating (which meant positively no use of the words spit-up, bowel movement or dangling drool) hoping no one would notice I was wearing my lime green prom dress. Being 100 percent polyester, it was stretchy enough to fit over my hips, and this time the top fit without the benefits of a padded bra.

I've been a mom long enough now to have recovered my old body. I don't have a baby to shop for any longer, but now I don't have time to shop. The good news is my lime green prom dress is back in style. And I took the blue and white striped knit dress and made a canopy for our beach trip this month.

✏ Pregnancy Tip

Do not, under any circumstances, take your blue jeans to the hospital in a totally misguided delusion that you can wear them home after the baby. This will not happen. Pack up those little sized jeans in a box so you can't even see them for several months. Take something comfortable and very stretchy to wear home.

✏ Pregnancy Tip

Forget the adage, "I'm eating for two." You are not. You are eating for one, plus one tiny fraction of a human. You do not need twice the number of normal calories. I promise you will thank me for this advice later, when the baby comes out, but the fat remains. There will be only one of you trying to lose the weight.

✏ Pregnancy Tip

If this is not your first child, when the older sibling comes to visit in the hospital, do not be holding the baby. Remember, this is a tough transition for the older one. It's like if your husband came home one day and said, "Honey, I love having a spouse so much, I've decided to get another one." Let the older sibling(s) have your total attention first before introducing the new member of the household.

Fantasy, Reality Clash
with
Birth of New Baby

Fantasies play an important role in our lives, fueling hope and helping us believe in the possibilities of the future. While pregnant with my first child, I attended a series of prenatal lectures at a local hospital. At one of them, a pediatrician spoke and showed us slides. "Now, I'm sure you have all contemplated your life with a baby," he said. "You dream of resting under the oak tree in the front yard, the beautiful baby sleeping peacefully by your side while you sip a cold glass of lemonade. Here is the reality." He flashed a slide of a screaming, red-faced, runny nosed infant with its tiny fists balled up in anger. It was a face, as they say, that only a mother could love. He was right of course, but at that point we were still caught up in our personal fantasies. "That won't be my baby," we all thought.

When the baby is born, that reality sets in even before the flowers you got in the hospital have died, but we don't lose our capability to fantasize. It's just that our initial fantasies change and we develop new ones. Here are some examples of mine:

Maternity Leave

Fantasy: Maternity leave will be a period lasting several months, consisting of blissful bonding with the new baby, and in my spare time, sewing balloon shades for my nursery, sending out engraved birth announcements with long letters to our out-of-town friends and finally organizing the photos from the past two years.

Reality: I have no choice but to bond with my daughter because she nurses for 45 minutes every two hours. However, blissful is not the word that leaps to mind when describing sitting on my couch for 10 hours a day with my blouse hanging open. There is little time left for anything else besides laundry and changing diapers. The birth announcements are the fill-in-the-blank ones my husband buys at Eckerd's and I find myself wishing I'd given my daughter a shorter name than Catherine Hamilton so I can get the blasted things done faster.

New Fantasy: Getting to take a shower and eat lunch in the same day, and possibly getting out of my nightgown before noon.

Marriage After Children

Fantasy: My husband and I will become a joyful family unit, more in love than ever as we sit peacefully at the dinner table, contemplating the beautiful baby we have created, and spending many happy hours dreaming of her future and ours together.

Reality: Peaceful dinners are a thing of the past, as my daughter thinks the initial clink of silverware on my plate is her signal it's time to nurse. Our dreams of her future are reduced to one: Let her sleep through the night. The three little words my husband and I now say to each other most often are "It's your turn!"

New fantasy: My fantasy involves men developing the ability to breastfeed. I'm not sure what my husband's fantasy is, but I notice that he spends a lot of time looking at the Victoria's Secret catalog, where the women don't have stretch marks and I'm sure never suffer mood swings due to postpartum hormonal imbalances.

Mothering

Fantasy: Although I know it will be difficult, I will maintain my composure and patience at all times and will never yell at my children, an act that can damage their delicate psyches.

Reality: In addition to their ability to be incredibly cute and adorable, children have the capability to make even the most patient person crazy at times, when they do things like hide the car keys in the dishwasher or throw your watch down the toilet.

New fantasy: That the doors and windows will be closed and the neighbors away when I discover things my children have done, such as dumping a five-pound sack of flour on the floor and trying to clean it up by spraying it with Lysol. The result is that my kitchen floor looks like a relief map of the Rocky Mountains and smells like the bathroom at the bus station.

Food for the Family

Fantasy: I will have plenty of time to focus on the nutritional needs of my family and will prepare complete, balanced meals every night the way my mother did.

Reality: There are days when finding the time to heat up a hot dog is a challenge.

New Fantasy: That McDonald's will add carrot sticks

to Happy Meals so I can pretend that they are nutrition-
ally balanced and that the Chick-Fil-A currently under
construction up the street opens soon.

I believe in the power of fantasy. It allows me to face
the future, knowing that in a few short years I will have
a teenager in the house. But I'm not worried. I know my
daughter will continue to be polite, maintain open communication with me, and never be embarrassed by anything I say or do.

Yeah, right.

✐ New Mother Tip
If anyone calls and wants to bring you food, by all means accept.
This is about the only time in your life, barring death or extreme ill-
ness, that many people will cook for you. Don't blow a good thing.
Remember, you've made your share of chicken casseroles in the
past. Relax and enjoy your turn.

✐ New Mother Tip
Don't spend too much time fretting about your body. Some of
those pounds really will melt off. It goes a little faster, however, if you
keep your hands out of the M & M bag. And many of us can expect to
hold onto a few extra pounds while we're nursing – only some of
which is in our breasts.

✐ New Mother Tip
These things are perfectly acceptable for a new mother: staying
in a nightgown all day, crying mysteriously, and not cooking for weeks.
At about the three-month mark, however, you're going to have to get
a grip and actually get dressed. (See next tip!)

✐ New Mother Tip
After a few months, get someone to baby sit and go shopping.
Just for yourself. Pack up those maternity clothes and find a few items
that fit you and make you feel good during this in-between stage
before your real body has re-emerged.

What to Expect
When You Least Expect It

I like surprises. I don't want to know what my Christmas presents are in advance. And I didn't want to know the sex of my children before they were born. I figured you needed something to look forward to after all that sweating, swearing and pushing. Finding out the sex of a baby is just the beginning of an unending stream of surprises that accompanies being a parent.

There are the everyday type of surprises that I have come to expect, such as the relocation of possessions – a toothbrush in the VCR, car keys in the dishwasher, and toilet paper encasing the dog. But there were also general surprises that I've never seen discussed in any parenting literature. I'd like to share three of the biggest surprises I have experienced as a parent.

Surprise Number One: I was shocked at how constant parenting is and how little control you have over you own schedule. B.C. (before children), a full-time job for me meant from 9-5 Monday through Friday with occasional evening activities. Outside those hours I could do other things as I pleased. Being a mom means being on call 24 hours a day. As my daughter said the other day, "Mom, you don't get a spring break, do you?" To expand upon that theme, there are no holidays, and no real vacations if children are involved. Anyone who has taken a trip with a baby or small child knows the true meaning of a working vacation.

A friend of mine once said that it would be a lot easier if children were like inflatable rafts. You could take them out on the weekends, drive up to the lake, drink a few beers and play with them. Afterwards, you deflate them and put them safely back in the closet until you feel the urge to play with them again.

Surprise Number Two: I didn't know that I would be the recipient of so much unsolicited advice and attention. From the time my pregnancy became obvious, it was almost as if my body was public property. People at parties asked me what I was drinking. It was only club soda with lime, but if I was in a surly mood I might say, "It's straight gin. How do you think I got knocked up in the first place?" I attended the Atlanta Food Festival when I was five months pregnant with my first child. A woman standing next to me reached over, put her arms around me and began rubbing my stomach. I'm still trying to think of what an appropriate response would have been.

Even worse was when I attended a Patron's Dinner at the High Museum of Art, where I worked. The museum director, Gudmund Vigtel, saw me just as I was getting off the elevator and stopped me to rub my tummy in front of the patrons, just as I was trying to act all sophisticated and stuff.

This is the same man, who when I was talking to his secretary and telling her I was pregnant, came out of his office and said, "Didn't you get my memo about staff workers not having sex?"

I don't like strangers or bosses touching me, but I endured that better than the unsolicited advice I received after my children were born. A woman in Service Merchandise looked at my son when he was just starting to walk and told me he would need corrective shoes. When my daughter was an infant, other mothers told me that I better start right then applying to the "right" preschools. I've been offered various other opinions on all aspects of child rearing. I take the L and I approach: listen and ignore.

Surprise Number Three: Parents have much less control over a child's personality and preferences than we'd like to believe. I now firmly believe that our children may be born naked, but they come equipped with a personality and a disposition all their own.

A few years ago I was talking with a male friend whose wife was expecting their first child. He had this child's life entirely figured out. His son (for he had determined it was going to be a boy) was going to have a wonderful life as a place-kicker. He would learn to kick a football in the backyard, shortly after he took his first steps. He would continue to perfect his craft, becoming a place-kicker in high school, leading to a college scholarship and then on to placekicking professionally.

I interjected at one point during the lengthy recitation of this plan to ask my friend, "What if he doesn't like football?"

"Well, of course he will, because we will make it like eating or sleeping. I will just be something he does every day, so he won't even know that he has the option of not liking it."

I didn't say much else, as I rarely give unsolicited advice, (see above.) I was much amused, however, when he and his wife went for an ultrasound shortly after this conversation took place. It was a girl. Now, years later, they are the happy parents of three more children. All girls. Not a place kicker in the house.

In the book, "Your One-Year-Old, " Louis Bates Ames writes, "every infant and every child is an individual, different in major respects from each other. Parents can help children fully express their positive characteristics and can usually discourage them from some of their less positive traits. But as a parent you can not determine what your child will be like."

In other words, they are not amorphous lumps of Play-Doh waiting for our guiding hand to develop them into whatever we want. Children are more like partially congealed grits. They have a shape, but with a lot of effort, can be remolded just a teeny bit.

So here is my rare bit of unsolicited advice: Expect the unexpected. Try and enjoy the surprises that having a child in your life can bring.

🖉 New Mother Tip
It is quite normal for you to often wish your new little bundle of joy would just shut the heck up and let you get some sleep. This does not make you a bad mother.

What's in a Nickname?

Endearment, humiliation and a lifetime of explanations

Next to the tinsel/no tinsel discussion over the first Christmas tree, there are perhaps no more heated arguments between couples than over what to name a child. We buy name books, research family trees and then engage in passionate, yet ridiculous name elimination games with our spouses over the selections: "I'm not too sure about the name Jake. Isn't that the name of the tennis pro you're always giggling over?" "Fine, I am definitely not even considering the name Ashley. You think I don't know that you had a crush on a girl named Ashley in 10th grade and you used to stay after school just to see if her skirt would fly up during cheerleading practice."

Then, after 99.9 percent of all possible names have been eliminated, a suitable name is arrived at by the deadline, the birth. (Okay, I confess, we missed the deadline by two days, and didn't name my daughter until we were leaving the hospital. We relented under the threat of the additional paperwork involved if you don't have a complete birth certificate upon discharge.)

All is well. Until the nicknames. And your darlin' little Stephen becomes Warty, Tom becomes Pimple Puss or Tinkerbell and Alexander Socrates Singer becomes, well, you can just figure out those initials for yourself, then add "boy" to the end.

Used as terms of endearment or surefire methods of humiliation, nicknames given in childhood can haunt us the rest of our lives. And you can't always blame it on the bullies in elementary school. My research shows that the worst nicknames come from your very own family.

There's the dad who called his daughter Little Stinky, his wife Big Stinky and his mother Super Stinky. And the loving sister of twins, confusedly named Sheryl and Cheryl, who called them Peewee and Fatso. Her mother made her stop the Fatso, so she changed it to Curly, but then her sister's hair got straight. Now the family calls her Chez, and Peewee, who is now a grandmother, is called Peezie by her grand kids.

Harry William Osborne Kinnard III has been called Crew since shortly after birth. His 11-year-old brother Bruce looked at him and remarked that the peach fuzz on top of his head looked like a crew cut. So he was known as "crew cut" by his siblings, which evolved into just Crew. My brother-in-law David had a big head, so he was naturally called Bobo Flat Face, which, mercifully, is usually shortened to Bobo.

One of my favorite stories was about a guy nicknamed Boys. He has about seven brothers, but whenever his mom would yell, "Boys, come to dinner," he thought she was talking directly to him. When he went to first grade and the teacher asked him his name, he simply replied, "Boys."

My daughter, tardily yet beautifully named, is now called Bones by her friends because she once wore a skeleton necklace at Halloween. When she was little I called her Pookie and Pookie Bear; my mother warned me that name might stick. After considering the potential social embarrassments and career limitations imposed on someone named Pookie Butsch, I stopped. She is now often known as Sweetie or Cutie, but only at home. My son is Doodlebug, but only when I wake him up in the morning. The rest of the day he is Buddy. Even our dogs have nicknames. Our first dog, Pepper, was most often called Pepperoni – or Devil Dog, on the days she was busting through the screens on our front porch or leaving half-eaten chipmunks around. Our dog Riley is called Roo Roo or Rooster.

Another rule of nicknames is that you can't really give yourself one. One of our friends wanted to be called Crash when he raced bikes in college. He was prone to exceptionally dramatic crashes, often involving loss of facial skin or consciousness and thought this nickname would capture his sense of adventure and make up for all that time he spent sailing over bicycle bars. "But it never really took hold," he said, and his best friend preferred to call him Jerk.

I also tried to create my own nickname. Despite my continued efforts, which often involved withholding food, clean socks, or rides to a friend's house, my kids refused to call me Best Mommy in the Entire Universe, for obvious reasons.

So for now I am nicknameless, which can be a blessed state indeed. Fortunately my nickname in college never followed me back to Atlanta from Virginia. I will only disclose that it had something to do with a plant that is native to the South, and had to be said with a drawling Southern accent.

Why Dads Shouldn't Nurse Babies

"Love them, just love them." Those are the last words in the Paul Reiser movie "Bye Bye Love," spoken by one of the fathers about children. This after he and his friends have dealt with sullen teenagers, vomiting toddlers and nine-year-olds that won't bathe. I nominate this comment for the Useless Parenting Advice Hall of Fame. It's like giving someone an airplane and saying, "Fly it, just fly it." We already know the basic concept; it's the method we're concerned about.

When my brother and sister-in-law were expecting their first baby, I wrote them this letter. It contains advice you won't find in movies or books.

Dear Chris and Julie,

At the beginning of December, your lives will change forever. I'd like to offer a few words of advice and encouragement. Chris, although you won't have to deal with the physical aspects of recovering from birth, a new father is under a lot of stress too. He is dealing with a new creature – one who has erratic sleeping patterns, is known to cry at the slightest thing, and is difficult to console. And then there's the baby.

Some dads want to help as much as they can. When

one couple we knew was pregnant for the first time, the father had a book called "Breast Feeding and the Father" or something like that. There's even a contraption that a dad can strap around his chest like a big bra, then he can insert a bottle in a hole so he get the breast feeding experience. The people who bought these are probably the same ones who bought those long funnels that you could place on the woman's stomach to talk to the baby in utero. In French. That way your baby could be born with the capability to order crème brulee in Provence.

Nursing is for mothers. Nursing a baby is sometimes the only chance a new mother gets to sit down. Besides, fathers are needed for equally important things, like getting her juice or a pillow, or telling her for the 87th time that she will one day wear her jeans again, and besides he loves her just as much with the 20 extra pounds and the additional chin.

Even when parenting an infant overwhelms you, don't forget your friends, especially the childless ones. It is difficult to do this because you have to a) remember what you used to do B.C (before children) b) try to carry on a conversation about it. When you talk to them, try to accentuate the positive aspects of parenthood. Remember – these same people who irritate you when they say that maternity leave is like a vacation are the same people who, if left unenlightened about the realities of tiny babies, may offer to baby-sit.

They are also your connection to the adult world, where people sleep all night and talk in complete sentences, which you will rejoin at some undetermined point in the future. Keep these friends or your social life may be reduced to visiting Chuck E. Cheese with people with whom you have nothing in common, except for the fact that you gave birth at the same time and both your babies get diarrhea when they eat strained peas.

Learn about child development. It helps to remember that babies are not rational beings. Years ago a man in my former office who was a new father came to work exhausted and frustrated.

"You won't believe what happened!" he said. "Last night the baby was screaming and I was going to change his diaper. I laid him on the bed and I told him that I was going into the other room to get a diaper. And he kept screaming!" He shook his head at the unbelievable irrationality of his son, who at this point was six days old.

The good news is that one day they do develop logical thinking skills. Then you can have enlightening conversations like the one I had with my son today after I picked him up from school. He was talking about waiting in carpool line.

"We told that girl to sit down and she wouldn't," he said.

"What girl was that?" I asked.

"The one that was standing up," he said.

I recently read a quotation by a woman named Elizabeth Stone that captured my feeling about being a parent. "Making a decision to have a child is momentous. It is to decide forever to have your heart go walking around outside your body."

See, the love part is easy. It's the every day things that you might need guidance on. Just don't look for it in the movies.

Love, Aunt Jan

Two

Bringing Up Baby

Baby Devices Monitor More Than Baby

Big Brother is watching you. Inside banks, even inside department store dressing rooms. Cameras gaze at you as you beg for an extra red lollipop at the drive-through window, or wiggle into that polka-dot bikini. Phone calls to some businesses are also monitored. And Prince "I want to live in your trousers" Charles can warn us how dangerous conducting personal affairs on a cell phone can be.

Most of us are aware of when and where we're being watched and govern ourselves accordingly. We wait until we get home to pry the gummy bears out of our teeth and adjust our wandering Wonder Bra.

One surveillance device is particularly insidious and intrusive. It broadcasts unsuspecting people's conversations, virtually without warning. And it could be right in the home of someone you know!

The baby monitor. That seemingly innocent device used by millions of parents to hear each coo, cry and cackle of their cherubs. While it is tremendously helpful, under the wrong circumstances the baby monitor can also be a source of extreme embarrassment.

My husband and I attended a christening party for our baby niece Claire in Texas. We are the godparents. The details of this responsibility are still being negotiated. My brother is holding out for full financial support or her education, beginning with preschool and ending when she has her doctorate. The exact amount of this support is unknown but hovers somewhere around the $878,235 mark, depending on whether snacks are provided free at preschool. My counter-offer is lots of toys and presents, my daughter's hand-me-downs and goofy stories about her father as a child.

Anyway, toward the end of the party, we went into the bedroom where Claire was sleeping to change into our traveling clothes for the flight back to Atlanta. We carried on a normal conversation, which may or may not, okay, it did, contain editorial comments about the other guests at the party. As I was getting ready to leave the room, I saw the small gray box with the bright red light on the nightstand. The baby monitor! Fear and panic struck me with equal force. I tried to remember every word we had said, wondering if the windows in the room were painted shut and if not, could we fit our suitcases through them for a quick escape.

Upon determining that escape through the window would be inconvenient, uncomfortable and perhaps just a tad on the rude side, we realized we had no choice but to exit through the bedroom door into the middle of the party. I went first, avoiding eye contact until I could locate the monitor's receiver and determine the extent to which our remarks had been broadcast. I found it in the kitchen. Lucy and Barney were there, but being members of the Canine-American population, they were easily bribed. We presented them with a few ham scraps and they pledged eternal silence.

Baby monitors are democratic. They transmit adult voices as well as children's. And you never know who is listening. One friend told me about turning on her monitor one day and hearing a neighbor yelling, "Okay, everybody, let's get naked!" The neighbor claims she was talking to the baby.

Of course, once you realize people will hear you if you speak into a baby monitor, you can use it to your advantage. For example, my daughter used the monitor for her confessions. The monitor was the priest and we were God. Catherine would come downstairs and make sure the receiver was plugged in. Then she would go back to her room and say, "Mommy and Daddy, I did something bad today." She would then detail her transgression, such as sneaking a cookie without asking. Then she'd go right to sleep, unburdened of her sin.

She also used it to voice her outrage at the restrictions of childhood. After coming downstairs one night after bedtime and promptly being sent right back up to her room, she expressed her displeasure to the monitor. "It's not fair! Grown-ups get to stay up late, eat Chinese food and watch movies. All I get to do is just lie here!"

Our baby monitor got the family a trip to the beach one year. When Catherine was just six months old we had a family celebration at my parent's house. One of my brothers asked my dad if he would rent a place at the beach for the summer. My father dodged the question, saying "I will rent a place when Catherine asks for it."

A little later I snuck upstairs and whispered into the monitor, "Grandpa, Grandpa, I want to go to the beach, please Grandpa!"

I think he knew it was me. But it worked anyway.

Tip For Little Ones

It does not matter when your child starts to walk. Pretty much all of them do at some point. It is not something to worry about, despair over or brag about.

Tip For Little Ones

Do not pay any attention to strangers who tell you your child will need corrective shoes, should be talking more, or should be wearing a hat/T-shirt/gloves in the winter. You do not need unsolicited advice from strangers, who for all you know keep their kids locked in closets. Just walk away!

Baby Brain Phenomenon Afflicts Moms

Many of you are probably familiar with an affliction I call "bride brain." It occurs in previously normal women going through wedding preparations, causing them to behave in a forgetful, scatterbrained manner.

While a woman can remember every detail of the 87 china patterns she looked at, she continually forgets her grooms' beloved dog's name, substituting the epithet, "that furry fellow."

Frequently, the groom panics at the prospect of being legally and eternally tied to a woman with bride brain. In severe cases, he may actually skip the wedding and head straight for the Caribbean honeymoon. Alone.

A week before her wedding, a friend of mine tried to tell someone where her reception was going to be held. "It's in that red brick house near Lindbergh Drive, up on that street, you know the one ...' she said, waving her hands in the air, her mind a total blank.

"Peachtree Street," I added helpfully, naming the

most famous street in Atlanta, where this woman had been born and grown up.

Fortunately, bride brain is a temporary condition, and disappears on its own, generally around the time the bride returns the first wedding gift.

A similar phenomenon occurs in women after giving birth. This condition is characterized by the same forget-fulness as bride brain. Unfortunately, its effects seem to last longer, possibly until late middle age, where it is renamed menopause, and there is no known cure. I call it "baby brain."

I myself am a victim of baby brain. Prior to giving birth, I had an excellent memory and rarely even used a calendar. Now I go to the drive-through at Wendy's, place my order, pay at the window and drive away. Fortunately, there is generally a small child with me who realizes that I neglected to actually obtain the food, which of course is the primary purpose of the fast food experience.

My guess is that fast food restaurants build baby brain into their profit margins, the amount even outdis-tancing the profit on French fries. See, sometimes a mom will drive all the way home without the food. After spend-ing 10 minutes getting everyone out of the car, she real-izes her mistake. At that point she has exhausted herself and her patience, so rather than getting everyone back in the car, she just spreads some peanut butter on a Pop Tart and calls it a McTreat.

My friends also admit having baby brain. Many of their incidents of forgetfulness involve vehicles. A woman I drove carpool with once told me she noticed a bad smell coming from her car, but was unable to detect its origin.

Finally, she discovered she had been driving around with a dirty diaper on top of her car for a week.

This same woman picked up my child for preschool one day. As she was driving away, I noticed a juice box perched on her back bumper. Later she told me it was still there when she got to school. I was so impressed with her driving skills, I thought about making this a test for anyone who wants to drive my children around.

An attorney friend of mine came to my house one day. (I mention the attorney part to demonstrate that women with baby brain are indeed still capable of functioning in the outside world, and even hold down jobs. Some contribute to society, and some are attorneys.)

After she left, I looked out my window and noticed her diaper bag lying in the road. When I retrieved it, I saw tire tracks on it. Not only had it fallen off the top of her car, but also she had run over it without even noticing.

I hesitate to publicize this phenomenon of baby brain, because it might damage the exalted position mothers have in the world. I say this facetiously, because in terms of respect, mothers of young children rank somewhere below Rodney Dangerfield and employees of the Department of Motor Vehicles. I am doing it so I can beg a little understanding – especially when commuters begrudge mothers using the high occupancy vehicle lanes. We deserve to use those lanes because we are victims of baby brain. We need those lanes to race back and retrieve our purse that fell off the top of our car four miles ago.

People used to wonder about the meaning of those "Baby on Board" stickers that were so popular a while back. Now you know – it means the baby is on board, but the dirty diaper is on the roof, the diaper bag is under the tires, and lunch is back at the Wendy's drive-through.

✏ Tip For Little Ones

To prevent catching fingers in car windows, have all kids put their hands on their heads before you roll up the windows. Also, tell them that the car does not go unless everyone is wearing a seatbelt or is strapped in.

☺ Web Wit

A small boy was sent to bed by his father. Five minutes later he called, "Daddy!"

"What?"

"I'm thirsty. Can you bring me a drink of water"

"No. You had your chance. Lights out."

Five minutes later, he called, "Daddy!"

"WHAT?"

"I'm THIRSTY. Can I have a drink of water?"

"I told you NO!" If you ask again, I'll have to spank you!"

Five minutes later, he called, "Dad!"

"WHAT!"

"When you come in to spank me, can you bring me a drink of water?"

Top Four Reasons I Want to Be a Kid Again

"I wanna be a grown-up," my four-year-old pouts; with his lower lip thrust out and down to his grape-popsicle-stained chin. "Dey gets to do everything!"

This was in response to my denial of a third Popsicle.

"Listen, I promise you, being a grown-up isn't that great," I said, probably setting the stage for years of therapy, maybe even a book – "Boys Who Won't Grow Up Because Their Moms Told Them It Was No Fun."

"We have to do lots of yucky stuff, like change diapers, and work for mean bosses, and wear clothes that feel bad, like stockings and ties," I said. "Our pajamas don't even have superheros on them. And if we go to a dinner party and they serve us gross food like Brussels sprouts and tomato aspic, we have to eat it or try to spit it out in a napkin and hide it in a plant."

"But you get to stay up late and eat dessert any time you want!"

I remember that feeling when I was a kid, thinking that grown-ups had it made. It was like they all had a conspiracy to get us to bed early, and then had a great big party every night doing secret grown-up things. I wasn't certain what it was, but I was pretty sure it involved a lot of candy.

The ironic thing is that when you grow up you don't even want to do some of the forbidden things anymore. I don't like to stay up late. I don't want to eat even one of those orange circus peanuts and certainly not a whole bag, a favorite childhood fantasy. Now I know that there is no party after the kids go to bed. Grown-ups lie on the couch, half brain-dead; watching the knitting channel because the remote control hasn't been seen since the dog dragged it away three years ago, and the channel button was broken by someone trying to change it with a broom handle. They are also fending off telemarketers by telling them they are saving all their money for a sex-change operation.

In fact, I can think of a lot of ways kids have it better than we do. Here are my top four reasons I wish I was a kid again.

Number One: Kids can amuse themselves and others endlessly with rhymes and making nonsense of the English language. "Windshield wipers, you wear diapers" is a phrase that can cause giggles for up to a week. Making up names is a constant source of hilarity, especially anything ending with "head." In our home, we allow this to a degree. That is, you can use the word "head," but it must be preceded by the name of a fruit or vegetable. For example, "pin-head" or "stupid-head" is off-limits, but "mango-head," "artichoke-head" or "rhubarb-head" is permissible. We try to work in five fruits or vegetables a day.

It is much harder when you are a grownup to get a genuine laugh out of another grownup. You have to actually be funny, be their boss, or be serving them massive quantities of alcohol in your house.

Number Two: Kids never worry about the Big Picture. Grownups worry about the Big Picture all the time. Kids only worry about the here and now. The future is an abstract and irrelevant concept. If you ask a child if he wants a Happy Meal right now or a VCR with all the Disney tapes tomorrow, the Happy Meal wins every time.

Kids are frustrated that they have to rely on adults to satisfy their needs, and adults insist on bringing things like values, setting precedents, and long-terms effects into a simple request like a box full of Twinkies for dinner. A kid doesn't care about sugar overload, the side effects of that mysterious substance in the middle, or what other parents will think about a diet of junk food.

Number Three: Kids feel no compulsion to be consistent. So what if you said you loved the chicken casserole your mom made last week, and said it was the best thing she ever made. That doesn't mean that this week you can't pronounce it totally disgusting and demand a hot dog instead.

Number Four: A kid can scream, cry, grab toys, pitch a fit and generally wreak havoc on everyone within a five mile radius, and her mother will look at others and say, "Well, she didn't get her nap today."

Grown-ups can't do this. We can't throw a Garfield coffee cup at the bozo in accounting who won't process our expense request because the receipt is ripped or tell the boss exactly what he can do with his demand for a budget by tomorrow, and then explain we're a little testy because we missed our nap. We are actually expected to be responsible for our behavior.

Of course, we could just be teething.

✐ Tip For Little Ones

No child ever died from wearing a stained shirt to the grocery store. No child ever starved himself. No parent ever died from being humiliated in public by a tantrum-throwing child, no matter how much we might have wished to sink into the floor.

Kids are messy, sometimes don't eat a thing except chicken fingers for days and are quite skillful at throwing public hissy fits. Life goes on.

☺ Web Wit

After the christening of his baby brother in church, Jason sobbed all the way home in the back seat of the car. His father asked him three times what was wrong. Finally, the boy replied, "That preacher said he wanted us brought up in a Christian home, and I wanted to stay with you guys."

The Problems with Balloons

Recently I was involved in a discussion about party decorations. "Just get a bunch of colored balloons, string them through a clay pot, and you've got a cheap and easy centerpiece," I suggested. One woman looked at me strangely. "I hate balloons," she said.

Hate balloons? How do you hate balloons, those colorful harbingers of cheer and festivity? Then I thought about it and realized I'd had some less than joyful experiences with balloons myself.

Latex balloons present their own particular problems. They are kind of like a short-term romance. Lots of fun for a short period of time, but don't count on them to stick around. Kids love those balloon animals you get at festivals and fairs. I've seen street performers make extraordinary shapes out of those long, thin cylindrical balloons. A few twists and they've got an entire Noah's ark, including pair of anteaters. The only problem is that after walking approximately 17 feet away, the balloons burst and disintegrate, followed immediately by similar behavior from the child.

My daughter got a kit with this same type of balloon for her birthday one year. "Amaze your friends!" the box said. "Mommy, make a poodle and a rhinoceros dancing together," my daughter said.

After popping about 20 balloons, causing increasing anxiety on both our parts, I finally got one to stay inflated, then tried to twist it in various places. After much wrestling while enduring those annoying high-pitched squeaks that only latex under stress makes, I managed to get one twist to hold together. "Look what I made," I said, proudly holding it up for my kids to see. They looked at it skeptically. "That's just a circle," they said disdainfully. "No, no, it's a snake eating its own tail," I said enthusiastically. They were not amazed.

There is a fun feature of helium-filled latex balloons – one that can liven up even the dullest party. Simply untie them, inhale the helium, and immediately your voice resembles that of Richard Simmons or one of the Chipmunks.

My husband once bonded with a high school friend of mine over balloon ingestion. We were invited to a party my friend was having many years ago. At the end of the party, they inhaled helium from balloons and did their impersonations of the munchkins from "The Wizard of Oz" singing, "Follow the Yellow Brick Road" over and over.

They quickly recognized in each other a level of maturity not often seen past the sixth grade. Thus was born a wonderful friendship. After also discovering their mutual love of music, they formed a rock band called The Yuppie Scum, and have now been playing professionally for over a decade. People pay them *real money* to play.

Occasionally they will repeat their helium-inhaling antics during parties where they are performing, especially if someone requests "ABC, As Easy as One, Two, Three" by the Jackson 5.

If latex balloons are good for short-term fun, Mylar balloons require a commitment. Those things have been known to last for decades, and are often passed from generation to generation. I bet if you looked in your grandmother's attic, you will find some "I like Ike" or "Repeal Prohibition" Mylars still drifting around.

Friends of ours were once wakened in the middle of the night by a frightening thumping noise coming from their kitchen. After a few scary moments, they called the police, who came rushing with guns drawn. They didn't need to use them, however. The balloon that was caught in their ceiling fan gave up without a struggle.

I got a Mylar balloon for my birthday one year. It said "Happy Birthday" and had a grinning Garfield on it. It was like one of those mariachi bands at Mexican restaurants – kind of fun at first but then you just want it to go away.

It seemed to take on human characteristics, skittering eerily across the ceiling, and following me from room to room for weeks. Garfield's cute smile turned into an evil leer. After an entire lasagna mysteriously disappeared from the kitchen counter, I decided that was it – I didn't care if the balloon was a present.

I got a pair of scissors and gleefully cut Garfield's tail off, released the air, and threw the limp and now powerless blob of silver and orange Mylar in the trash.

I banned Mylar balloons from our home for years. But then we had children, and they love balloons. On Valentine's Day I bought one of those huge ones, with a big red heart on it. It was about the size of our first house. The next day my daughter decided to take it outside and set it free. At last sighting it was approaching Jupiter. And I had so looked forward to passing it down to my grandchildren.

I never did find out why that woman hates balloons. Perhaps it was a scarring incident from childhood involving a water balloon. But I still love them. As long as they don't have a face.

✐ Tip For Little Ones
There is no right or wrong way to cut a sandwich.

✐ Tip For Little Ones
Plastic scissors with rounded tips are great for youngsters, but remember, they still cut. My neighbor gave her three-year-old a pair to play with during a car trip to cut up construction paper, only to turn around a few minutes later and find out that she had decided to cut her hair instead.

☺ Web Wit
A physician had a four-year-old daughter. On the way to preschool, the doctor had left her stethoscope on the car seat and her little girl picked it up and began playing with it. "Be still, my heart," thought the doctor. "My daughter wants to follow in my footsteps!"

Then the child spoke into the instrument: "Welcome to McDonald's. May I take your order?"

Heaven Help the Younger Sibling

I was at Fellini's, my favorite pizza place, the other day and saw a young woman with a baby in a high chair enjoying lunch with her friend. Her child dropped his Winnie-the-Pooh teething ring on the floor, and without even taking her eyes off her friend or interrupting the conversation, the woman scooped up the drool-infested ring and tossed it back on the tray of the high chair. With that one swift movement, I knew this was not her first child.

Parents of multiple children claim to love them all equally. That may be true. But I'll bet you a lifetime supply of Snoopy band-aids that no one can claim to treat him or her the same, especially in the first few years of life. Here are some examples:

Pacifiers. First child: If the first child uses a pacifier, it is treated with all the deference of a DNA sample and is kept in a pristine, sterile environment at all times. Should it fall on the floor, the parent scoops it up immediately, and if a stove is available, will sterilize it thoroughly in boiling water before reinserting. If a stove is not

~ent will rinse it off in the sink under
: or she can stand without screaming,
vill eventually be necessary.

:he pacifier falls on the floor, the par-
. ιc up, perhaps wipe it on a napkin, or possi-
˛ ˛pit on it and wipe it off on a shirt, and give it back
to the child.

Third child: The child throws his pacifier across the
room. Mom kicks it across the floor to Dad who picks it
up and reinserts. Any large clumps of dirt or dog hair
may or may not be removed.

Baby Monitor. First child: Monitor is turned on at all
times and the receiver is permanently attached to the
mother's body. When she is in the shower, she places it
in carefully in a Zip Loc bag next to the shower and turns
the volume to its upper limit. She buys clothes not for
their fashion appeal, but because they have loops on
which she can hook the monitor.

Second child: The monitor may or may not be turned
on, and the receiver batteries can be dead for weeks without anyone noticing.

Third child: What monitor? By this point the parents
have figured out the baby will survive crying for a few
minutes before being picked up, and that it is not really
necessary to sneak into his room every 15 minutes and
hold a mirror to his mouth to make sure he is still
breathing. Parents will engage in yard work, outdoor dinner parties, and various other activities for hours at a
time, relying on any available older child to report a
change in sleeping status.

First Birthday Parties. With the oldest child, the

first birthday may involve an extensive guest list of friends and families, engraved invitations, a new, carefully selected outfit for the birthday child, and at least seven rolls of film. The sofa will be recovered and the kitchen cabinets repainted prior to the big event.

The second child generally has a party, maybe with a few friends from playgroup, and a cake.

The mother remembers the third child's birthday that afternoon, sticks a candle on her corn dog at dinner and the family sings "Happy Birthday."

Pictures. Every smile, frown, laugh and cry of the first child is recorded on film and a new room is added to the house to hold the photo albums.

The second child is still fairly well photographed, although the number of baby albums is dramatically reduced and all the baby photos may actually fit into one album.

The third child will inevitably grow up and inquire one day, "Was I adopted into this family at a late age?" Some enterprising mothers have been known to take the two existing baby photos of the third child, have copies made, and insert them into appropriate places in the family photos, prompting comments such as "Wow, look, Uncle Joe is holding me there at the Shriner's Convention, and I thought he died before I was born!"

As young parents, my husband and I were no exception. When my daughter was a baby, we lived in a house so small we had only one phone and could reach it from anywhere in the house before the second ring. Yet I would not even go into the next room without the baby monitor, although her cry was loud enough to be heard in Chattanooga. Going to the mailbox was a production in itself. I check the baby, checked the batteries in the monitor and ran the approximately 17 feet to the mailbox and back, just in case something happened in the 12.87 seconds I was out of the house.

We moved into a bigger house when I was pregnant with my son, partly to make room for the 87 photo albums of Catherine. We lined them up on the shelves and organized them with titles such as "Catherine Sleeping on Side" "Catherine Spitting up to the Left" "Catherine Spitting Up to the Right" and "Trips to the Park – the Autumn Series."

My son does have an album. His, however, is simply marked "Christopher."

When my brothers each had their first babies in the same year I prepared their first holiday gifts. I got the Pacifier Sterilization Chamber, 187 rolls of film, batteries for the monitor, and a bookcase to house the photo albums.

☺ Web Wit

A mother was preparing pancakes for her sons, Kevin, 5, and Ryan, 3. The boys began to argue over who would get the first pancake. Their mother saw the opportunity to teach a lesson. "If Jesus were sitting here, He would say, 'Let my brother have the first pancake, I can wait.'" Kevin turned to his younger brother and said, "Ryan, you be Jesus!"

Shop Till You Drop

Goals of grocery shopping change
when you have children

One exhausting thing about having children is that you have to feed them *every day!* If you don't believe me, just try skipping a day and see how much whining you can stand.

This means lots of trips to the grocery store. It the old days, B.C (before children), I was an organized shopper. I clipped coupons out of the Sunday paper, made a list, and often achieved my goal of only going to the story once a week.

After having two kids, my goals have changed. Gone are the organized list, the coupons, and the time spent at the checkout counter taking the "Are Your Eyebrows Flirty Enough to Attract Mr. Right?" quiz in the latest issue of Cosmopolitan. My goals now are:

1) Leave all the toys in the car. I once had to walk up and down every aisle in the grocery store, retracing our steps, to look for a red plastic missile the size of a toothpick. We miraculously located it in the cleaning products

aisle, where my son probably dropped it while I compared the scents of the lemon versus the pine toilet bowl cleaners. By that time, the $3 melting box of popsicles was leaving a rainbow-colored trail of slime through the store, and the $6 chicken breasts in my shopping cart were probably quietly collecting salmonella, but we found the 35-cent toy.

2) Try to keep the same cart. Many times I've been zooming around the store, usually in search of some obscure item like white truffle oil from some dish I'll never actually make because I dropped the recipe in the grocery store, totally oblivious to the increasingly insistent calls of "Hey lady, that's my cart." It's really embarrassing when they have your cart, and one of your kids is still in it.

Once I wheeled someone else's cart halfway throughout the store and only discovered the error because we had had Ralphie the dog sitting in the cart. When Catherine discovered his absence, she wailed out, "Ralphie!" A bewildered man who had come to the store alone, and was now pushing around a cart with a stuffed dog, walked over and we made the exchange.

3) Remember to close up the packages of food we've opened before we check out. Because a shopping trip with children can take several hours, you have to replenish with a few snacks along the way. It is a little embarrassing when you check out with half a box of Chex Mix, three juice boxes missing out of the pack and the chocolate icing licked off a box of doughnuts.

Once we bought a bag of Raisinets and ate several handfuls. Not realizing it was open; the checkout clerk whisked it across the bar code reader, sending a shower of chocolate-covered raisins everywhere. I'm sure she still has some stuck to the bottom of her shoes.

We also try to remember to pay for bakery items we've eaten. My daughter is helpful in this area. She will yell out, "Mommy, don't forget to tell him about the two cream-filled, sprinkle-covered eclairs you just ate!"

4) Have the food arrive home somewhat intact. My son sits in the cart and makes towers and hideouts for Batman out of the canned goods. Somehow the bread always ends up underneath the 28-ounce can of tomatoes, so we're used to odd-shaped sandwiches. One day he came home from a friend's house and said with amazement, "Mom, they had *square* bread!"

Once, when he was a baby, Christopher opened up the egg carton and amused himself by dropping the eggs, one by one, on the floor. I am ashamed to admit that when the clerk came to clean them up, I pointed at him accursedly and said, "He did it!"

5) Review the merchandise prior to entering the checkout lane. As the children have gotten older, they've gotten craftier about sneaking in the Double Frosted Super Hero Sugar Bomb cereal, carefully hiding the box under the low-fat granola bars, and whipping it out at the last second. They know at that point I've reached a point of exhaustion where I am up to a verbal chastisement, but have no energy left to actually extricate myself from the line and return the box to the proper aisle.

6) My last goal is to arrive home and actually have food for dinner. Many times I have bought everything I needed for snacks for soccer, school lunches, quick

breakfasts, and a cake I was making for the neighbors. While I am unpacking the multiple bags, my kids ask, "What's for dinner?" And there is nothing.

I either pull out a can of Chef-Boy-R-Dee ravioli left over from a food drive last fall, or tell them it's Orange Food Night. The menu? Cheez Whiz on carrots and circus peanuts for dessert.

✎ Tip For Little Ones

When a child brings a drawing home from preschool, do not guess at its subject, as we are apt to guess wrong, resulting in hurt feelings or righteous indignation. Simply say, "Tell me about it."

My son once brought home a blank piece of white paper and told me it was a picture of all of his friends in a snowstorm.

✎ Tip For Little Ones

Family Fun is a wonderful magazine for moms of younger children. It is filled with clever, affordable craft ideas and easy recipes. Visit the web site at www.familyfun.com

☺ Web Wit

We child-proofed our home, but they are still getting in.

Games Grown-Ups Play

How spouses compete for 'The Worst Day' title

There's a game played by millions of Americans every weekday. It doesn't have a name, but if you've ever been part of a household where one spouse went to work while the other stayed home with small children, you'll recognize it. It's called "Who Had the Worst Day." Here's an example of a typical day.

(Disclaimer: I know women go to the office and men stay home; I often begged for such an arrangement in my own home years ago, but I've used the most common example of the wife at home and the husband at work.)

9:00 a.m.

Wife: You've been up for three hours, but haven't had time even to comb your hair. The kitchen is a wreck, and you stare angrily at your husband's half-full coffee cup in the sink. You picture him with another cup of coffee lounging in the hallway at his office, sharing the latest joke with his co-workers, and admiring the short skirt of an account executive, who spends at least 30 minutes a day on her hair. You're sure she flips it flirtatiously at your husband several times a day.

Meanwhile, the baby needs to be changed, the phone is ringing and you still haven't had time to go to the bathroom.

Husband: You've been up for three hours and no one has said a kind work to you yet. Your wife grumbled, "umph" when you left because she had the baby's dirty T-shirt in her mouth while she was changing a diaper, and the parking lot attendant yelled at you for parking in the wrong section. Then your boss appeared at your door and demanded a report by the end of the day.

You think longingly of your home, where you picture your wife rocking contentedly with the baby, in between engaging in a tea party and reading "The Cat in the Hat Comes Back" with your 3-year-old.

12:00 p.m.

Wife: You wipe off the half-chewed peanut butter sandwich pieces from the high chair, eat the leftover Cheese Balls for your lunch and pick up the entire box of Cheerios that spilled when the 3-year-old insisted, "Me do it!" As you walk to the refrigerator, you slide on a piece of blackened banana, which becomes embedded in your house shoe (you still haven't had a chance to take a shower and change your clothes). You imagine your husband sitting in some elegant restaurant. He gets to have someone else make his lunch, serve it to him and clean up after him. He will get to eat sitting down!   And not one person will mention bowel movements, rectal thermometers or anything to do with nasal excretions.

Husband: The phone hasn't quit ringing, your computer has a virus, and your assistant is being snippy. While the computer is restarting, you run down to the cafeteria, grab lunch and eat it at your desk, dispersing breadcrumbs into your keyboard and spilling tomato soup on your white shirt. You think enviously of your wife at home, having a picnic on the back deck with a few friends while the children play in the backyard.

2:00 p.m.

Wife: After countless more diaper changes and a bottle, you finally get the baby to sleep. The three-year-old, who is vehemently opposed to naps, is content with a video for a few minutes, so you race to take a shower and finally get dressed. You step in, and feel the blessed relief of the warm water.

Husband: You miss your family and have about two minutes before a conference call. You call your house.

Wife: The phone rings. Worried it might be a repairman who is coming to look at the washing machine, which has been broken for a week, you jump out of the shower. The baby, awakened by the phone, starts crying, and the 3-year-old yells for some juice.

"Hello?" you say.

"Hi honey," he says.

"What do you want?" you say.

5:00-7:00 p.m.

Wife: As you enter the 13th hour of the routine? Feed the kids, clean up after the kids - you look at the clock, which actually seems to be moving backwards, and wait for your husband to get home from his cushy job.

Husband: You finally finish the report for your boss, who absolutely had to have it today, and find out he has gone to Hawaii for a week. You go to the parking lot, where the attendant glares at you and seems to laugh at your tomato soup-stained shirt, and get in the car to fight the traffic. You arrive home wearily.

Both: "You wouldn't believe the day I've had."

They share details, but neither sympathizes with the other. The husband is actually jealous that she didn't get dressed until after noon, and the wife would give anything to eat lunch sitting down by herself, even if it is at a keyboard.

To counteract these miscommunications, I'd like to suggest a new concept: instead of Take Your Daughter to Work Day, we need to have a Let Your Spouse Do Your Job Day. We'd all get along much better.

☺ Web Wit

One summer evening during a violent thunderstorm a mother was tucking her son into bed. She was about to turn off the light when he asked with a tremor in his voice, "Mommy, will you sleep with me tonight?"

The mother smiled and gave him a reassuring hug.

"I can't dear," she said. "I have to sleep in Daddy's room."

A long silence was broken at last by his shaky little voice: "The big sissy."

☺ Web Wit

A little girl asked her mother, "Can I go outside and play with the boys?"

"No," her mother replied. "They're too rough."

The little girl thought about it for a minute, then said, "If I can find a smooth one, can I play with him?"

Dealing with Children's Questions

Without actually having to know the answers

I've developed a lot of skills in my years as a parent. Some are useful for everyday life: I can get ready for a party in two minutes flat, pulling on stockings, stirring macaroni and cheese for the children's dinner and applying Torch Lily lipstick simultaneously. Some skills are rarely in demand: I can take a pipe cleaner, a tissue and a piece of paper and construct anything from a sailboat to a tulip to a wedding veil for a Beanie Baby.

One useful skill I've acquired is the ability to handle the approximately 187 questions my children ask me every day, without actually knowing any of the answers. These questions cover topics such as "What do butterflies eat?" and "Why doesn't Winnie-the-Pooh ever wear any pants?" and "Why do they put words on the outside of airplanes when they fly too high for you to read them anyway?"

These are some strategies I employ:

Deflect the question. It took me most of my adult life and many weeks of reading "Miss Manners" to learn that you don't always have to answer a question. One way not to answer it is to deflect it. For example, my daughter asks, "Mommy, what is the oldest tree in the world?" And I respond, "Did you know that in China, if someone tells you you're one in a million, there are a thousand people just like you?" After she is through pondering whether it is beneficial or detrimental to have a thousand clones, and checking my math, she has forgotten the original question.

Use an older child to answer. The other day my son asked how rocks and minerals were formed. Before I could even start to dig through my memory files to form a decent response, my daughter started in about lava cooling and explaining the origins of the different types of minerals. Now I know when my son asks me a difficult question, particularly about geography, a category I never pick on "Jeopardy," I can pretend like it's a teaching opportunity for my daughter.

Use those three little magic words. Say, "I don't know." I really don't understand parents who hate to admit they don't know something. To me, it's quite a liberating expression. Not that I revel in my ignorance, but confessing my lack of knowledge tends to put an end to that particular line of questioning. (Although I have to admire their persistence because they still never stop asking.)

A lawyer friend of mine never says, "I don't know." He probably learned that on the job because it's hard to charge $250 an hour if those words ever come out of your mouth. He always says, "I can't speak to that," implying that while his body of knowledge about the universe is vast, it doesn't happen to contain that small fragment of obviously unimportant information.

Offer to look it up on the Internet. You can't lose with this approach. You can either have fun finding out together what butterflies eat for lunch and maybe even find out the dining habits of the praying mantis as well, or the child gets bored and goes outside to play. Then you can surf the Net, picking out restaurants to try when you take that fantasy trip to the Greek Isles to meet the new buddies from Zanzibar you've been e-mailing.

Answer "Because he/she thinks it makes them look good." This response can be used to cover a large portion of a curious child's questions, which they tend to ask in an extra-loud voice. In public. These include: "Why did that bald man spray brown paint on his head?" or "Why does the waitress have 12 earrings in her left ear, and one on her tongue and what happens to the one in her nose when she gets a cold?" or "Why does Aunt Wanda shave off her eyebrows then draw them back on?"

Make up an intriguing answer. My daughter asked why there are only 24 hours in a day. I told her there are only 24 hours in a kid's day, but after kids go to sleep, grown-ups all get together and have a big 10-hour party every night, so we actually have 34 hours in our day.

Laugh. Sometimes it's the only response. Which is exactly what I did when my son asked me this question recently: "Mommy, the man who invented the first watch, how did he know what time it was?"

A Proliferation of Plastic

Organizing toys a massive, barely rewarding task

Plastics, the future is in plastics. That's the advice given young Dustin Hoffman in the 1967 movie "The Graduate." Hoffman's well-meaning advisor also accurately predicted childrearing. The future has arrived and is covering every square inch of my house.

It was the week before Thanksgiving. My in-laws were coming for the holiday, and I was also hosting my book club right before their visit.

I needed to paint the bathroom, make a shower curtain, plant flowers, plan menus and iron the kitchen window treatment, which I had washed back in the summer in a rare bout of cleaning frenzy. (The frenzy gave out before I put it back up, however, and it had remained in a wrinkled heap since June.)

In the spirit of procrastinators everywhere, I decided to embark on a totally unrelated project. Organize the toys.

I enlisted the whole family and we pulled all the toys from every crevice in the house with the intent to organize, recategorize, prioritize and garbagize. We discovered Mr. Potato Head lips behind the chair in our bedroom, super hero laser launchers under the couch, Littlest Pet Shop monkeys in our cubbyholes in the kitchen and enough McDonald's Happy Meal toys to include in meals for children in the state of Idaho for an entire month.

As I looked at the melange of molded plastic pieces of Kynex, Legos, Lincoln logs, action figures and Barbie shoes, I was filled with regret at starting this ridiculous task in the first place. I found myself wishing one of the following would occur:

My house would burn down. (Yes, I know it's drastic, but it would free me of the guilt I feel when I toss out my kids' artwork.)

I could just move, selling the house to a family with small children and putting in the sales contract that as a bonus, all the toys were theirs, for free!

I could quickly build a basement and just toss the toys down there and ignore them, figuring when my kids were teenagers, they would be so excited about the prospect of having a make-out spot they would clean it up themselves.

But after dreaming of escaping the fiasco, realism intruded.

After much tedious effort, the Lincoln logs, Kynex, army men and Legos were finally segregated and neatly organized in toolboxes from Home Depot. The Toobers and Zots were reunited in a yellow mesh bag. The toys to be given away or donated were in a large box. The trash man came and took away three huge bags with unsalvageable remains, such as a checkerboard torn in half with only three checkers left. (My son is still pouting about that one. "We can just use Sweetarts for checkers," he cried. We had tried that once, but my "checkers" kept mysteriously disappearing.) Another trashed item included the father doll from the dollhouse family who had lost his right leg in a domestic accident years before. Although we located the leg, our efforts at reattachment were unsuccessful. We hated to get rid of him, but the mom doll didn't seem too upset. Last I saw, she and Ken were cruising down the hall in Barbie's convertible.

If you are insane enough to think about attempting such a project, I suggest you sit down, drink a cup of hot tea, and read *Vogue* until the urge passes. But if you just can't concentrate on your own spring wardrobe while your kids are complaining that Barbie is forced to wear the top from the Malibu collection with the pants from the ski ensemble, or that Batman has to walk everywhere because his cape and the control to his Batmobile are missing, I offer a few suggestions.

Although you want to enlist your children's help during the project – because it's all their fault in the first place - I do not recommend it. If they don't participate, the broken, never-played-with toys can be discarded discreetly and the kids will never miss them.

If the kids do help, you will hear outraged shrieks of "But that's my favorite toy!" which is yelled with equal passion for a miniature pinball game that has lost all its balls and "My Little Pony" that had all its hair cut off, but has been wearing Darth Vader's head piece to cover the bald spots.

Toss the broken toys into a large opaque trash bag.

Slip it into your trash bin. Even better, if your neighbors are gone, slip it into theirs.

Wear shoes. If you've ever stepped on a Lego or a metal jack with bare feet, I don't need to elaborate.

And if you're a little overzealous and practically deplete your supply of plastic and are faced with empty shelves, don't worry. It only takes one birthday party; one visit from the grandparents or a few trips to McDonald's to replenish your supply.

☺ Web Wit

Zachary, 4, went screaming out of the bathroom to tell his mother he'd dropped his toothbrush in the toilet. So she fished it out and threw it in the garbage. Zachary stood there thinking for a moment, then ran to her bathroom and came out with her toothbrush. He held it up and said with a charming little smile, "We better throw this one out too then, 'cause it fell in the toilet a few days ago."

☺ Web Wit

A little boy opened the big family Bible. He was fascinated as he fingered through the old pages. Suddenly, something fell out of the Bible. He picked up the object and looked at an old leaf that had been pressed in between the pages. "Mama, look what I found," the boy called out.

"What have you got there, dear?" she asked.

With astonishment in his voice, he answered, "I think it's Adam's underwear!"

☺ Web Wit

A little boy was overheard praying: "Lord, if you can't make me a better boy, don't worry about it. I'm having a real good time like I am."

A Day in the Life of a Five-Year-Old

Corn Chex for breakfast again. Mommy won't buy any good cereal like Fruit Loops or Sugar Pops. She says we might as well eat a bowl full of sugar. Sounds good to me.

My big sister is at school. I love my big sister. She is my best friend. I only have one sister. But sometimes Mommy says she is raising three kids. I don't know what she means, but she usually looks at Daddy when she says that.

I ask where Daddy is. "He's at the office," Mommy says. I don't know why he goes there all the time. Mommy says he goes to make money, but I never see him bring any home. All he brings is a big briefcase every night that he puts by the front door, and Mommy says, "Can't you put that somewhere else? This is the only room in the whole house without junk all over it.' But it is always there.

He has gum in his briefcase. Mommy won't let me chew gum since the day she found a wad of it stuck in my jeans pocket. It's not fair. After all, she was the one who told me not to throw it on the ground.

Mommy says that after school Luke is coming over to play. He's my best friend. Mommy is telling me to get dressed. "I've asked you five times." A lot of times I see Mommy's lips moving but I don't hear anything. I think Daddy has the same problem.

I don't understand why you have to keep changing your clothes anyway. You go to bed, you change clothes. You wake up, you change your clothes. You go to church, you change your clothes. Mommy is the one who always complains about laundry. Why can't we all just be like Winnie-the-Pooh and just wear the same shirt all the time? He doesn't even wear pants, so it's much easier.

I play blocks with Jack at school. He is my best friend. I play with Annie on the playground. She is my best girlfriend. I am going to marry her. But there will be no kissing. Kissing is way yucky. Mommy kisses me all the time. I wipe off all of her kisses, except the one at night.

Luke comes with me after school to play. I got some peanut butter on my hands. Mommy says not to wipe it on my shirt, so I wipe it on the bottom of the chair cushion. Luke gets jelly in his ear. I don't tell him. Mommy says jelly attracts bugs and I want to see if any ants crawl in his ear.

We play trucks and aliens. Luke wants the Queen Alien, but it's the most awesome one and I don't want him to have it. I yell at him, "You're not my best friend!" Then I call him a buttstack. I'm not sure what that means, but it's fun to say and it makes him mad.

Luke and I make up. He goes home. I put on my

totally cool Batman costume Mommy made me for Halloween. I do a few Batman kicks and practice beating up the whole world. I sneak up and play on the computer, a way cool game Daddy got where you shoot bad guys. Mommy doesn't like me playing it, but I only shoot bad guys. She catches me, and I run and hide under the bed and cry. I find a gummy bear under there from Halloween. It isn't too fuzzy, so I eat it.

My sister comes home. I run down the street to meet the bus. I try to give her a hug, but she swings her book bag at me. I hate my sister.

Mommy takes me to the drug store. I meet a little boy in the candy aisle and we make farty noises with our underarms and laugh. I don't know his name, but he's my new best friend.

Bath time. I make a huge fuss and yell, "I don't want to take a bath!" Then I get in and I don't want to get out. Mommy says she doesn't understand, but it makes perfect sense to me. When I'm out, I don't want to be in. When I'm in, I don't want to be out.

I pour the whole bottle of bubble bath in and I have totally awesome bubbles. I can even make tunnels in them for the Red Ranger to attack that dorky rubber duck.

Bedtime. Daddy reads books to me and tickles me. Mommy and Daddy give me a hug. Parents are so weird. Every night, no matter what bad things I did, Mommy says she loves me and that I am her favorite boy in the whole world.

She will be so happy tomorrow when she finds the marshmallows I put in her orange juice.

Three

School Days

The Great Divide

Mothers differ when it comes to carpool

No more wearing a plastic visor with a childish scrawl on it at Mom's Day. No more trying to think of a nutritious snack that starts with 'Q' to correspond with the letter of the week. (I bought quail eggs, but realizing their limited appeal for preschoolers, settled for a quarter of an apple and a quintuplet of goldfish crackers.) School starts this month, and for the first time in seven years, I won't be a preschool mom. With little fanfare beyond a lunch at Three Dollar Café with his buddy Andrew, my youngest graduated from preschool last May.

I have lots of fond memories of our years at preschool. But there is one thing (besides the tuition) I won't miss: carpool line.

What was once a fairly quick expedition became a lengthy exercise in stress management this past year as major construction began on my son's preschool. The usual two lanes of carpool were merged into one, the construction workers parked their vehicles on both sides of the road, and on occasion the line just quit while a huge piece of equipment lumbered slowly out of the parking lot. Large cranes often dangled huge pieces of pipe or other metal contraptions perilously over the roofs of our cars. The line snaked around the parking lot like a motorized version of Candyland, backing up into the side streets.

Occasionally unsuspecting souls would find themselves stuck in line. I often saw a look of panic on the face of a non-carpooler as he or she came into contact with this mysterious cult, which seemed to require owning a mini-van with bright yellow plastic numbers displayed prominently on the front windshield.

When I first began driving carpool, station wagons were the car of choice. I fit right in with my recently purchased, six-year-old Volvo. Then the minivan craze hit. Beyond the comfortable ride they offer, minivans have the added benefit of being able to hold all the children from your entire zip code. Then you only have to drive carpool once every odd-numbered year.

I've found there are two types of carpool drivers. There are those of us who sit staring vacantly at the "I Love My Jack Russell Terrier" bumper sticker on the car in front of us, pondering if we can avoid a torturous trip to the grocery store by taking the leftover chicken and green beans in the refrigerator and adding some sun-dried tomatoes and artichoke hearts, thereby producing a Martha Stewart-esque dinner that our husbands will admire and the children won't even feed to the already-waddling-from-previously-unpopular-meals dog, and wondering whether the kid we drive who has been practicing belching his ABCs will ever get past the letter 'G.'

Then there is the second type. This group is composed of women whose homes seem to run with Swiss-like efficiency. You know the kind – women who have coke cans lined up in the refrigerator with all the labels facing the same way in order by expiration date; sheets neatly folded and placed on the expertly coordinated-to-match-the-wallpaper shelf paper in the linen closet with labels for which bed they belong to; and pristine coffee pots in which they brew freshly ground coffee and through which they run vinegar the first Friday of every month.

I'm sure they even have a list of nutritious snacks that start with every letter of the alphabet, even Q. These women don't have to worry about stopping at the grocery store, because they go every Tuesday at exactly 11:15 a.m. with their computer-generated list of the items they need for exactly the number of meals they'll be preparing.

These women are not ones to waste the time they spend sitting in carpool line. They have learned how to perform pedicures, make hand-painted Kleenex holders for teachers' presents, clip cereal coupons, and pick out upholstery fabric for the living room couch, all while continuing to maneuver through the carpool maze.

I once saw a woman making grilled cheese sandwiches with a skillet that connected to a cigarette lighter. These women accomplish more while sitting in carpool line than I do during my entire spring break.

Every one of them has a cell phone, and if they are not performing any of the above feats, they chat. I'm certain they are arranging an exciting afternoon, and I'm sure it doesn't rival mine, which will consist of scraping congealed Spaghetti-Os off of my kitchen counter.

This year I am not driving carpool. Instead, my husband will drive carpool to the elementary school in the morning and the school bus will drop my children 10 feet from my front door in the afternoon.

I think the bus driver must also be a survivor of the preschool carpool line. I saw her sewing a skirt while she waited for the children to get off the bus.

✎ Tip for School Kids

To make a peanut butter and jelly sandwich for your child's lunch that doesn't become soggy during the day, spread a thin layer of peanut butter on both pieces of bread, then put the jelly on one side.

☺ Web Wit

A woman invited some people to dinner. At the table, she turned to her six-year-old daughter and said, "Would you like to say the blessing?"

"I wouldn't know what to say," the girl replied.

"Just say what you hear Mommy say," the woman answered.

The daughter bowed her head and said, "Lord, why on earth did I invite all these people to dinner?"

Express Yourself - But Not in *That* Outfit

"**M**om, I can't wear this," my friend's daughter wailed. "It just isn't me. I look ugly. If I wear this I will have a terrible day all day." Was this a hormonal teenager worrying about what to wear on the first day of school?

No, it was a five-year-old despairing about her outfit for a day at kindergarten.

The issue of clothes can be an explosively divisive one in the parent-child relationship. Every morning the same conversations are taking place all across the country. "Just wear this!" "What happened to all those cute dresses I bought you?" "I don't care what the other kids at school are wearing, you are not going to wear that!" "I know it's your favorite shirt, but it has holes in it!" "I don't care if Wilson wears the same shirt every day with a basketball-sized hole in the armpit."

There are many books published about fostering creativity in children. Parents love to inspire their children's imaginations, and gloat over their creativity and artistic creations. The irony is that, when children wish to express themselves through what they wear, heated battles may ensue. We value self-expression. We just don't wish to see it manifested in hot pink polka-dotted leggings with a chartreuse tube top or a black Megadeath T-shirt.

Why is it so hard for us to let our children dress freely? Maybe because when they are born we have total control over what they wear. It can be hard to give that up. It can also be hard to hear our taste is less than awesome.

"I bought her $400 worth of darling clothes at Parisian. I had to return every bit of it," laments one mother about her six-year-old daughter. "She told me the clothes just weren't cool."

Parents can feel that they are being judged by how their children look. I used to be embarrassed when my husband sometimes dressed my children on weekends to take them out to lunch. He had a talent for pulling out the clothes that were too small, and mixing them in interesting combinations – a navy and red jumper with a royal blue and white striped shirt. Pants that came up to my son's shins. Plaid shorts and flowered shirts. I would fight to remain silent and remind myself that it was nice to have someone else dress them, and the important thing was that they were spending time together. My husband didn't care, my children didn't care, why should I?

Other parents have foregone the clothing battle. A mother in my parenting class said that her son wore a short-sleeved purple T-shirt every day for two years. One of the strangest attire stories I heard was about a couple in South Carolina whose son wore a mixing bowl on his head every day throughout preschool.

Every family will experience conflicts. One of the keys to cutting down on them is to determine your priorities and let other things pass. I figure that the issue of clothing is a battle I don't need to fight. Letting my children wear what they want doesn't hurt anybody, isn't hazardous to their health as long as they are dressed warmly enough. My son wore his black fireman hat, black plastic fireman vest, and yellow rain boots every day for months. I liked it because it was easy to peel off half-eaten fruit snacks and wipe up spilled fruit punch.

I do have a few basic rules for my children: it has to be clean, they can't be improperly exposed and they have to wear nice clothes to church. I admit it is easy to say because I have a daughter who will basically still wear what I buy, and a son who rarely notices what he is wearing. But I know the day is coming when my daughter will probably wear faded jeans and baggy T-shirts, and do who-knows-what to her beautiful long hair. I hope when those days come that I can be accepting and maybe even admire her self-expression, whatever it may be.

When my son was in kindergarten, he decided it was a good idea to sleep in his clothes. So after his bath, he put on clean pants and a shirt. At first I protested, then realized that this was a good thing indeed! It was one less thing to do in the morning, as he woke up all ready to go, and as far as I've heard, a few wrinkles never interfered with the learning process.

A few years later, after collecting several T-shirts from his summer camp, he began wearing the same thing every day: khaki shorts and a summer camp T-shirt. Again, I had no complaints. I was in one of those dreaded communal dressing rooms recently. A woman was with her teenage daughter who was trying on pants. The mom told her that what she bought was up to her. Then she asked how her belly ring was doing. I saw in the mirror that the girl had a small silver hoop hanging off her navel. Now that is an accepting mom.

I was at church a few years ago on a cold day in February. There was a little girl on the playground wearing a shirt and pants, with a one-piece bathing suit on top of it. In this case it was hard to determine whether these were very accepting parents or just exasperated ones who said, "Okay, fine, wear your bathing suit to church. Just get in the car."

It's good to eliminate some battles because there will always be more important ones to follow. Like getting them into clothes at all. My daughter marched down the stairs this morning as we were frantically getting ready for church, announcing loudly, "Christopher says he is not going to get dressed. He is in his room and says he is never coming out."

Tip for School Kids

If two kids are sharing one item such as an apple or a piece of cake, ward off those cries of "Her piece is bigger than mine!" with this simple step. Have one child cut the item in half and the other get first pick.

Hacking Up Sugar Cane

And other field trip fun

A big advantage of having children is that you get to do fun things you did as a child all over again. And some of those things have gotten even funner. Like going on field trips.

When I was in elementary school I remember only one field trip the entire eight years. To the Atlanta Zoo, which was not the beautiful, animal-friendly facility it is now. At that time animals were mostly kept in cages, including Willie B. who didn't know yet that he was a gorilla, and spent his days watching TV, ignoring his tire swing and spitting at visitors. (We *were* intrigued by his behavior, and I think a few of my classmates adopted him as a role model.)

My Brownie troop went on field trips too. Once we even got our picture in The Northside Neighbor newspaper. We went to Mathis Dairy and milked Rosebud the Cow, a rite of passage for children in Atlanta in those days. Our photo was in the paper with the caption, "City Girls See Cow."

My favorite Brownie field trip was to the Frito-Lay factory. (Haven't you ever wondered how pork rinds were made?) We got to see potatoes being sliced razor thin for chips, and at the end got a bag of Frito-Lay products. We must have been working on our nutrition badge.

At my children's school, the minimum number of field trips per grade is three, and the kindergarten year is essentially a series of field trips occasionally interrupted by some schoolwork. Not that I'm complaining. Children learn a lot from field trips. I expanded my knowledge as well, and in some cases acquired skills that will serve me well in everyday life.

I learned how to hack up a piece of seven-foot long sugar cane with a small dull Swiss army knife. I had gone to the State Farmer's Market with my daughter's kinder-garten class. Each mom was given a few dollars and four children to watch. We were told to wander around the stalls and pick out fruit and vegetables to purchase and taste.

Unfortunately my crew was not satisfied with easily divisible or sliceable items such as grapes and bananas. They wanted to taste that sugar cane, which was as hard as a flagpole. I tried each of the multitudes of knife blades, after abandoning hope there was a tool just for sugar cane when I realized there is very little sugar cane grown in Switzerland and it is doubtful that the army was ever confronted with hacking through a field of it. I was finally able to make a dent in it with the corkscrew and then gnawed at it with the teeny scissors. Finally I was able to cut a small chunk for each child. They chewed on it for a few seconds, spit it out and ran to find a watermelon the size of a tractor for me to cut up.

I yearned for that knife on our trip to Imperial Fez Moroccan Restaurant for lunch later that year with the same kindergarten class. In Moroccan style we had taken off our shoes and were lounging on the floor on pillows around the tables. The children were delighted when they found out we got to eat with our fingers, but the waiter didn't tell me how to divide a Cornish hen among five children using my hands, while alternately breaking up the inevitable pillow fights.

On a trip to Stone Mountain for a hayride and cook out, I learned that hay has an amazing ability to creep up your pants and settle in really uncomfortable places. And it is very sharp. If I were a cow or a horse, I'd keep looking in those fields for something more appetizing. After the hay ride was the wiener and marshmallow roast and I learned that it is possible to give 87 small children a pointed stick, let them run around with abandon and *no one gets their eye poked out.*

And it was on field trips I first learned my name at school is not Jan or even Mrs. Butsch, it's Catherine's Mommy or Christopher's Mommy.

So to continue my learning process this year, I will again sign up to chaperone as many field trips as possible. And if anyone ever asks if I am involved in my children's school, I can show them the ticket stubs from the circus and my white turtleneck that is now encrusted with glitter from supervising crafts at The Art of the Season. And of course, my scar from the sugar cane incident.

The Secrets That We Keep

Don't tell kids about dancing the polka

"**M**om, did you ever have a mohawk?" my daughter asked me while driving in the car a few weeks ago. This was a question that did not require any thought before I answered, unlike many she has thrown my way, such as, "Do you have to be married to have a baby?"

"No," I replied truthfully. "Why do you ask?"

"Well, I saw this commercial. I think it was about gum. It had this test to see if your parents were cool."

"Sorry, I don't think I can qualify on that one." I have always been rather conservative with my hair. I don't think it is fair to count the time I turned my hair Bozo-orange after an unfortunate encounter with do-it-yourself highlights. That was a mistake. I decided not to tell her about that. But I was concerned about the direction of this conversation. This was a child that until recently was impressed by my ability to roll my tongue, make bunny birthday cakes and Mickey Mouse pancakes, and hop the length of our family room on one foot while balancing a bean bag on my head. Now it seemed that I was up against an entirely new set of standards.

"You and daddy did get points because it asked if

your parents had ever been to a heavy metal concert, and you and daddy went and sat on the third row!" she said with great delight.

Actually, it wasn't heavy metal. It was a Rolling Stones concert, but hey, when you're cool you don't sweat the details. And I could tell we were getting coolness bonus points for sitting in the third row, which was the result of total luck when I picked a number at Publix to get tickets.

"And you don't dance the polka," she said smugly.

Uh oh. Her dad is safe there, as far as I know. But I do admit to one incident of polka dancing when I was in my twenties. I had gone on a retreat with a volunteer organization of the High Museum of Art. During one of the breaks, several of us slipped away to scenic Helen, Georgia (motto: like Europe, but with a putt-putt course and an outlet mall) and visited the Old Heidelberg Inn. I confess I drank a few beers, and polkaed my heart out with a young lawyer who shall remain nameless. He has political aspirations and I would not want this polka incident to tarnish his image. In some circles, a polka in your past is worse than unpaid nanny taxes.

Personally, I love the polka, such a happy, bouncy dance. The tango may be more sophisticated, but the dancers always look so pained. As if their undergarments were a tad too tight. I decided not to tell my daughter about the polka in my past, as it would obviously distress her. Besides, I didn't inhale.

"It's not really cool if you go bowling," she continued. "You just went once, but that was for daddy's birthday. I think that's okay."

For my husbands 35th birthday I had the traditional surprise Mexican food/bowling/karaoke party in his honor. After fajitas at U.S. Bar Y Grille, I gave everyone their choice of rub-on tattoo and we hit the bowling alley. I like bowling. I like the democratic way we are all reduced to wearing the same shoes. No pretentious footwear allowed.

Following that was my first and only experience with karaoke. Several of our group got up and sang. Then one friend chose "Should I Stay or Should I Go" by The Clash. Five of the women, including me, got up to sing back up and be Do Wop girls, long a fantasy of mine. However, I began laughing so hard I couldn't even perform my best moves, focusing primarily on not wetting my pants. I wondered if that would be considered cool. I think not.

"Yeah, I think you did pretty well on that test," my daughter concluded happily.

Maybe she was happy but I wasn't. How could this be happening already? We had gone from being All-Knowing and Wonderful Parents to this – being judged against the standards of a *gum commercial*. Sure, we passed this test, but what about the next one?

It also bothered me that I wasn't being open and honest with my children. Now here I was, shading my past. Hiding the polka incident, not being technically truthful about the heavy metal concert. Was I on a downward spiral of deceit?

Maybe I'll come clean when she's a little older. After all, she was pretty forgiving about the bowling. If all else fails, I can always get a mohawk.

Laughter is Not Always the Best Medicine

"It's not funny!" my son yelled angrily. I had giggled at some remark he made about school. "I'm not laughing at you, I'm laughing because you're cute," I said, infuriating him further. "I am not cute!" he protested with all the indignities that a five-year-old can muster, running out of the room.

"Hey, I can laugh if I want to," I called after him, demonstrating all the maturity of a six-year-old.

Then I thought, what am I teaching my child? That we can laugh whenever the mood strikes us? I pictured him, 20 years from now at an interview for his dream job, which if he follows his current career path will be as a weapon-making, cape-wearing super hero moonlighting as a firefighting prince. "Mr. Butsch, you would be perfect for the job," the interviewer is saying. "However, when you laughed at your prospective boss' face at lunch when his toupee fell in the split pea soup, we decided that you may not possess the necessary social skills for the job."

My kids need to learn that we don't have the freedom to laugh whenever we want. Sometimes it is inappropriate or embarrassing to express our amusement. I speak from experience.

One such incident occurred when I participated in sorority rush. My college had allowed women to attend just a few years before and sororities didn't yet have houses, so rush was held in the basement of fraternity houses.

I had been in a lot of basement family rooms in my life, but experiencing a fraternity house basement in the daytime, completely sober, is something for which you can't really prepare. Dark paneled walls; the ripped, beer-stained pool table top mended with duct tape, and a crumpled copy of Cliffs Notes for *MacBeth* stuck under one leg to make it level; the maroon, fake leather couch, also held together with duct tape; the faux wood-grain bar decorated with neon beer signs; the dusty beer bottle pyramids in the corners; the beer-stained, peeling, brown linoleum floor, over which you must move quickly or risk being permanently stuck.

The main floor of a fraternity house often borders on being presentable, but the basement maintains its own personality – a shrine to beer and duct tape, those two items so dear to a man's heart. The smell of stale beer, old sweat socks and cigar smoke added to the ambiance, recalling ghosts of keg parties past.

The sorority girls were valiantly trying to ignore the atmosphere, serving us punch and cookies and chatting with us. Then they all formed a circle and started singing, in a most serious tone, a song about love, sister-hood, friendship and maybe even kittens. While they were singing, I looked down a hallway and saw what I had discerned had formerly been a pair of blue-striped boxer shorts hanging on a bare light bulb protruding from the wall. They had melded to the bulb from the heat, looking like a Salvador Dali-inspired lampshade.

I began to giggle and then laugh out loud. I tried to fake a cough, but didn't fool anyone. The singing sorority girls glared at me. They didn't invite me back.

Another time my family was in St. Louis attending mass at my husband's family's church. My husband, who had been entirely silent the entire time, not even repeating any of the responses and prayers which I know he knew by heart because he had attended Catholic school for 87 years, decided to participate in the singing portion. The priest sang, "The Lord be with you," to which the congregation is to sing, "And also with you."

My husband decided to belt it out in a deep Tony Bennett-meets-Bill-Murray kind of lounge singer voice, accompanied by a dramatic hand gesture. He looked like he was addressing a couple at a nightclub celebrating their 20th anniversary by taking in a show and drinking too many sloe gin fizzes.

I lost it. I started laughing. In church. In front of my in-laws and all the other devout St. Louis Catholics.

I tried to hold it in by taking deep breaths and doing aerobic facial contortions, forcing my lips together, but then I just ended up snorting through my nose like a wounded goose. I tried to think unfunny thoughts, like how I was going to have to spend 10 hours in the car with two small children the next day, or perhaps eat tomato aspic at lunch. Even that didn't work.

So here I was in the situation of trying to teach my

children about self-control, a skill that I hadn't mastered myself. I went to my son and told him I was sorry and that I shouldn't have laughed at him.

Later that night as I was fixing dinner, I squirted mustard on my white linen blouse. My kids laughed and pointed at me. "It's not funny!" I said. "We can laugh if we want to!" they shouted in unison.

At least they didn't say, "We're not laughing at you; we're laughing with you." I had tried that on my son one time, to which he responded, "How can you be laughing *with* me when *I'm* not laughing?"

✏ Tip for School Kids

Find a place in your house and designate it as the "fuss bench." It can be a sofa or a stair or just anyplace you can fit two kids. When kids are fighting and want to draw you into the conflict or are just irritating the poo out of you, send them to the fuss bench. Then each child has to tell what he or she did wrong, not what the other one did wrong.

At first you may get responses such as, "I didn't hit him hard enough" or "I got caught." After you get a real answer, then lead a discussion on how they could have handled it better. You will probably find that they will eventually begin to work out conflict on their own rather than make a trip to the fuss bench.

Surviving the
Homework Blues

"**T**here are three words that no one should ever be allowed to say: 'I like homework,' " my son ranted recently.

"Do you really think we should tell people what they can say?" I asked, despite the fact that I learned long ago it is fruitless to try to inject reason into the ravings of a 9-year-old.

"Well, there are zillions of words in the world, and they can say any of the others they like," he reasoned. "Just *not those three*, or they should go to jail."

Fortunately for the future of the First Amendment, I doubt my son will ever actually be in the position of making such a law. But his words do reflect his utter disdain for any activity that causes him to a) pick up a pencil, and b) possibly miss the all-brand-new-but-I've-seen-it-three-times-and-it's-my-favorite-Pokémon TV episode.

With the start of the school year, the biggest adjustment for our family is not getting up at a ridiculously early hour (ridiculous being defined as any time where the first number on the clock is anything less than a 7), figuring out which carpool line to be in, or even what to pack for lunch. It's surviving the daily grind of homework.

"The thing I hate about homework is that you have to do it at home," my son grumbled another day as he stormed out of the car and into the house, disgruntedly dragging his backpack through my begonias. I didn't even bother to respond to that one. Logic plays no role in the life of a frustrated child.

I learned that one day when I was equally or possibly more frustrated over the daily homework hassle. "If you spent half as much time *doing* your homework as you do *fussing* about it, we wouldn't have a problem," I said.

He stared at me blankly. The concept that one should consider the time factor involved in the amount of fussing one does was beyond him. Complaining, much like sleeping, is a necessary function of life and limiting it is of no value whatsoever.

So I tried to institute a no-fussing-about-homework rule, (despite my total lack of success with a similar rule at dinner.) Now instead of broadcasting his feelings to the world at large about the utter uselessness of composing a sentence with the word 'twitch', he just puts his head down and mumbles. My curiosity gets the better of me. So I say, "Did you just say you'd rather be at the bottom of the ocean getting crab bites on your behind than sitting here doing your homework?" We then have a 20-minute discussion of what I thought he said, what he really said, and why was I listening when he was just talking to himself when I could be doing something productive, like making pepperoni pizza for dinner.

I've tried to understand how he felt, but it really hit

home one day. It had been a trying afternoon. He had left his math book at school and we had to track down another one, borrow it, and return it within a 45-minute span.

As he was heading to bed that night, I asked if there was anything else he had to do. He thought for a moment and said, "Well, one teacher said to bring lima beans tomorrow, but I think she was kidding."

We then discussed whether his teacher could have been serious, and if she was kidding, what's so funny about lima beans, and why hadn't he told me earlier.

After much deliberation, I decided it was better to be with lima beans than without. As I wearily headed out the door to go back to the store, both kids came running out. "Mom, I need you to fill these out," they both cried, thrusting stacks of papers in my hands. Clinic forms, emergency contacts, directory information, field trip permission slips.

With my plans for a well-deserved relaxing evening in front of my newly reinstalled cable TV, perhaps watching beavers at play, shot, I headed out the door.

I stocked up on M&Ms and popcorn, came home, and sat down at my kitchen table with my snacks and my large stack of homework. "I *hate* homework!" I thought. "Don't these teachers even care that I got homework from all the other teachers?"

But then I tried to look on the bright side. I already knew all the answers to the questions, I wasn't getting graded and, assuming I could locate the dentist's phone number and the kids' social security numbers, I wouldn't have to pull an all-nighter.

The Leader of the Band

When my older brother was in preschool he came home one day very excited.

"Mommy, I've been chosen to be the leader of the band!" he cried.

"Wow, Greg, what an honor," my mother said. "How did that happen?"

"Well, the teacher asked all the kids who could sing to raise their hand. And they did. Then she asked all the kids who could play an instrument to raise their hands, and they did. And I was the only one left!"

Although my brother did go on to develop musical talent and is a gifted guitar player, the rest of my family remained chronically musically challenged. The traditional singing of "Happy Birthday" sounded like the honkings of a herd of really cranky elephants, and to this day continues to be a rather painful occasion at our family parties. Although my husband and two children can carry a tune, the voices of my father and me are enough to butcher even the sweetest notes they may find.

I was reminded of my own struggles to accept my lack of tune-carrying ability recently when my son came home with a note from school saying that everyone was going to be purchasing recorders, an instrument for which I hold a great fondness. When I was in elementary school we had a chorus. Every day Mrs. Puett would lead us in our spirited renditions of such favorites as "America the Beautiful" or "Who Will Buy" from the musical "Oliver" with the bad words "I swear I could fly" changed to "I think I could fly" and I would enthusiastically join in.

But then one day we sang the song, and then she said, "Okay, everybody. Let's try that one again, but this time Jan, you just listen." Then they would all sing it again, while I stood there just watching, confused as to what I was supposed to be getting out of this curious exercise.

After several days of me just listening, Mrs. Puett kindly suggested that maybe I'd like to try recorder lessons. Now, there were a few boys playing the recorder, but no girls. And we all knew that it really meant that you were being kicked out of choir. And to be the only girl kicked out of chorus was not a thing to aspire to.

So I rather reluctantly got my recorder. Then I fell in love. After starting slowly with "Mary Had Little Lamb" I quickly moved to a stirring rendition of "Kum Baya" and a rousing arrangement of "Bicycle Built for Two." I regained my confidence from my undeniable talent and the emotional resonance I was able to project in my melodic renderings of "Love Story." The highlight was when I was able to impress my friends with the theme song from "Green Acres."

I told my son this story and he said, "Well, that makes

sense. Not everyone can sing. But everyone can blow."

So I adjusted to my propensity to remain off-key, and consider lip-syncing an act of kindness to those around me when public singing is required. On a recent vacation I was on a cruise ship, enjoying the live band during a Sail Away party. Out of the hundreds of people present, the lead singer shimmied over to me and held the microphone in front of my face to sing the chorus of Gloria Gaynor's "I Will Survive." I hated to disappoint her, but there were not enough strawberry daiquiris on that entire boat to get me to open my mouth, so I just smiled at her. It reminded me of an old saying that goes something like, "Better to be thought a fool by remaining silent, than to open your mouth and remove all doubt." For the rest of the trip, I just pretended I was from Brazil and didn't speak English.

I loved it when my children were infants because I could sing to them. Every night we'd sit in the rocking chair, and I would sing softly, usually the same three songs, "Twinkle Twinkle Little Star," "Baa Baa Black Sheep" and that mockingbird song, you know the one about the diamond ring turning brass. I like to think I helped spur their language development – my son's first words were "Mommy, please don't sing anymore."

The lesson from all this and what I try to teach my children is that we can all be a leader of a band. It's just a matter of figuring out what band.

Happiness in a Little Yellow Bag

What ordinarily was a routine late-afternoon visit to the grocery store took a turn for the better when my son and I made an amazing discovery in the frozen food section: waffles with chocolate chips.

"Whoa, look at this!" I said to Christopher. "Let's try these."

As he rarely ventures outside his four food groups of chicken tenders, pizza, macaroni and cheese, and hamburgers, he was skeptical.

"Come on, how bad can they be?" I said. "They have chocolate chips in them."

The stock guy, who I am sure has overheard his share of amusing exchanges, got a kick out of that. "For breakfast?" he chuckled.

It has been my unstated policy, at least until now, that virtually anything is improved by the addition of chocolate chips, and I consider the chocolate chip muffin one of the greatest inventions of the 20th century. Plain old banana bread is elevated to a new culinary level with this simple addition. My friend Melissa even throws a handful on her breakfast cereal. "It's a great way to start the day," she says.

Many other things have come in and out of my life - men, jobs, friends, houses and clothes (with the exception of that ratty yellow terrycloth robe from the Carter administration that I still wear.) But one thing has remained constant. The power of the chocolate chip.

When I was growing up one of the first things I learned to cook was chocolate chip cookies. Page 83 in the Betty Crocker's New Boys and Girls Cookbook, from 1965. (We still have that cookbook, although pages 82 and 83 are now stuck together from years of dropped cookie dough.)

I became quite skilled in chocolate chip cookie making, and was not above using this talent to my advantage. It's probably safe to say that a few guys I went out with stuck around a little longer than they would have just to eat a few dozen more. And when I no longer considered it worth the effort to measure out the brown sugar to make cookies for them, I knew the relationship was over.

When I was a volunteer for the High Museum of Art and had to sell memberships, I coerced several coworkers into writing that check with my limited-time offer of a dozen cookies with their paid membership.

However, because I've always had to watch my weight, I was unable to totally indulge my taste for all things chocolate chip. Until I became pregnant. At which time I justified my once-a-day cookie or ice cream indulgence with the age-old "craving excuse." For a few blissful weeks I thought I was getting away with it. Then at the routine weigh-in at the obstetrician's office, I was horrified to learn that I had gained eight pounds. In three weeks. After that I had to curb the craving.

One of my favorite indulgences was introduced to me by my neighbor, who works for Piece of Cake. One Christmas she brought over a chocolate chip pound cake. The recipe goes something like this: Take two pounds of butter and 18,700 chocolate chips. Mix and bake at 350 degrees for one hour. Give each family member one slice. Cut up the rest of the cake into pieces, hide it in the freezer and tell your family it's all gone. (I added that last part.)

Fortunately for them, my children have not inherited some things from me - my Mr. Magoo-vision or my inability to color in the lines. But luckily for them, they have inherited my love for, and my belief in the power of the chocolate chip. No matter how bad things may seem, life always looks a little brighter after eating something, anything with chocolate chips.

By now some people are probably thinking that my love affair with the chocolate chip borders on addiction. That may be so, although I believe I could stop any time I wanted. I just don't see the need to try. Especially tonight: We're having chocolate chip fajitas for dinner.

✏ Tip for School Kids

When your young children protest about leaving home when it's time for college, make them this deal. "If you reach 18 and you still want to live at home, you will be welcome." Trust me, it won't be a problem.

Pet Denial Lands Mom
in Mean Category

It's official – I'm in the running for Worst Mother of the Year in the Pet Acquisition Denial Category. And we're not even talking about a pony, a dog or even a cat. Yes, I confess that I wouldn't even let my child keep a goldfish. But before you start dialing in your vote for me (1-800-MeanMom), let me defend my position.

When my daughter, Catherine, was two years old, she got a goldfish at a birthday party, which in my mind, wins the award for worst birthday party goodie ever, readily beating out the sharp swords that one mother gave out to 18 six-year-old boys who took turns stabbing each other in the car on the way home. The next day we went out and bought $87 worth of supplies for the free goldfish. We put the bowl on the kitchen table.

Catherine paid attention to it for about three minutes, but when she learned it couldn't go for a walk or do flips on command no matter how loudly she screamed at it, she quickly lost interest.

Meanwhile, like one of those paintings whose eyes follow you around, that goldfish seemed to stare at me everywhere I went. And its lack of activity began to bother me.

I knew I had entered a danger zone when I found myself talking to it, asking, "How can you stand to just float around all day?" and "Don't you have any goals?" We had two dogs and they didn't seem to suffer from lack of activity. Their days consisted of two main activities: eating and sleeping, with small slots of time allotted for slobbering, drinking from the toilet and barking at squirrels. (They reminded me of a guy who lived next door to me in college, except he usually drank from a beer keg.)

Anyway, a few days later I found the goldfish floating at the top of the bowl. I soon realized it had not learned a trick, but was deceased. We performed the usual flush-it-down-the-toilet ritual, and I packed away the bowl and year's supply of chemicals and fish food.

So when my daughter came home from a school fair recently, excitedly clutching a clear plastic bag filled with water and one small goldfish, I was unable to share her enthusiasm. I assumed it would have just as much ambition as its predecessor, and would hold her interest only slightly longer. She of course had no recollection of its goldfish predecessor and was not happy when I told her I didn't want to keep it. She gave it to her friend, Lindsey, who last I heard, managed to keep this one alive for several years, which proves to me that it went to a much better home, where it probably didn't die rather than face the constant stress of living.

We've had our share of other pets. There was the Year of the Expiring Rodent. For some unknown reason, except that maybe he had spent too much time around chemicals in the garage, my husband decided to take the children to PetSmart, where he bought three longhaired hamsters and a large five-bedroom condo for them, complete with exercise wheel and a Richard Simmons tape. I resigned myself to our new housemates, although I was a little jealous. How come they have more bedrooms than we do? But they seemed low-maintenance, except for their propensity to escape. Our family became adept at concocting rodent-catching devices, which usually involved shoeboxes, peanut butter, string and several hours of time.

We also had one of those plastic balls to put hamsters in and they are supposed to amuse themselves by running around the house. I don't know how amusing the poor creatures found it to be used as bowling balls, hurled down the hallway at speeds rivaling that of light.

Unfortunately, the hamsters died one-by-one of wet tail disease, so we cleaned out the cage with Clorox and bought a pair of gerbils. Apparently, some of the bleach fumes remained and affected their lungs, and they also met with an untimely demise. The three mice we bought to replace those did well for a while, and then they also passed away from unknown causes. At that point, we decided to hang it up for a while, before we added several species to the endangered list.

A far better route to go in the pet category is to borrow them. That way you can have all the mess, frustration and hassle with none of the expense and the guilt. My children's school has more animals than most city zoos. The children are allowed to bring them home for weekends and vacations. One year we hosted some type of creature almost every weekend – mice, birds, rabbits, gerbils and hamsters.

One year, we had the rabbits, Ebony and Nickels, for almost a week during Thanksgiving. Despite our efforts to clean their cages regularly, it smelled terrible. Not even our pumpkin pie smell could penetrate the Eau de Lapin. I threatened to make Fatal Attraction Stew for Thanksgiving dinner.

At that point, we did have a dog. Her name was Trixie and we bought her from the Atlanta Humane Society. She was 13 years ago, which made her 2,387 in dog years. The kids realized that she might not be around much longer, so they started asking about getting a puppy. I think they were secretly taking lessons in pet acquisition techniques from my daughter's friend. She was at our house a few months ago and said, "I heard my parents talking last night and I think they finally agreed to get me a puppy. They said 'Let's go ahead and do it so she'll stop whining about it so much'." She added, "I thought about whining for a pony but it seemed a bit much."

Although my resolve to not get a puppy is strong now, I have a feeling I may lose this battle. What is a mother's "no" compared to three pairs of pleading eyes, two children's voices begging, and one wagging tail? I probably should have let my daughter keep the goldfish. At least it wouldn't chew up my new family room couch.

Our Priceless Treasures Aren't

The hidden costs of raising kids

Recently I read yet another report about the astronomical cost of raising a child to the age of 18. The new figure, which I don't recall exactly but it had more digits than my phone number, is actually an erroneous estimate. It didn't even include the cost of tube socks.

That's just the beginning. Here are several more items that weren't included with the cost of education, clothing and food. (I also doubt that the cost for clothing included pajamas from Limited Too, Abercrombie & Fitch shorts, or tennis shoes that cost more than the monthly rent on my first apartment. Fortunately for the budgeting of food costs, the price of a slice of pepperoni pizza from Fellini's has remained relatively stable over the past few fiscal years.)

Here's just a few of the items not included:

Hobbies and Trend Following

Counted in this category are any trends or hobbies your kids are into. The pleas for money to purchase these items generally contain the phrase, "All the other kids have them – do you want me to be a nerd?" Examples in my household have included:

• The key chain trend a few years ago. Kids purchased multiple key chains to put on their backpacks. While parents initially applauded a trend they could follow for $1-$2 each, when they multiplied this by the 387 key chains, then by the number of children they had, the costs escalated quickly.

• The Beanie Baby fad. At last count, our household contained enough Beanie Babies to give at least one to every child in the states of Alabama, Mississippi and half of Tennessee. At an average cost of $5 each, they represent a large portion of our investment portfolio. The good news is their value has held up better than our technology stocks, and they are so darned cute.

And let's don't forget the trading that ensues after they own the coveted items, which often leads to additional expense. Once relegated to front stoops and schoolyards, the advent of the Internet has now expanded a child's ability to trade his items with other kids over the entire planet. This is bad, bad, evil news for parents. A man I know has a son who loves hockey. His son discovered the joy of eBay, and was lucky enough to place the winning bid on several hockey-related items. And his dad only had to write 28 checks to cover his hobby.

Fundraising

My kids have been good at selling goods to raise money for their school or scout troops. But thanks to the prize system, they always need to sell "just a few more, please, Mom!" to get that adorable stuffed werewolf or the miniature boom box, without which it seems their ability to live will be severely impaired.

Consequently, I purchase my weight in Girl Scout cookies every year and have enough wrapping paper to gift wrap my house.

Replacement Costs for Damage to Household Items

Always unforeseeable and therefore extremely difficult to budget for, items in this category include these real-life examples (fortunately not all my life):

• New contacts to replace the ones your two-year-old fed to the dog.

• A new paint job for your van, required after your five-year-old put his hands in the fresh white paint in your bedroom and made handprints all over the side of your new red Windstar.

• New carpeting for when the Kool-Aid stains can no longer be covered up by the artful rearrangement of furniture in the family room.

• Fabric and re-upholstery costs for when you asked your 8-year-old to watch the group of younger children in the living room while you served dinner to company. He did as you asked: He watched as they tested his new markers on the white brocade fabric.

Batteries

If you have kids, no further explanation needed. If you don't, let me explain by telling you that if the number of batteries we've gone through were all still working, we would have enough energy to light all the hotel rooms in downtown Atlanta. At least for a couple of years.

But lest we parents get discouraged, or non-parents decide to remain that way, let me say that having kids is like those MasterCard commercials. You can add up all the expenses you incur by having them, which is a thoroughly depressing exercise, but think about one bear hug, one jelly-faced kiss, one outstretched hand reaching for yours or one "Mommy, I love you." Priceless.

Which is more than I can say for the crystal lamp in the dining room, which got broken last week during an indoor game of dodge ball.

✏ Tip for School Kids

I heard somewhere that parents make four mistakes a day on average. (Where do they come up with this stuff and what qualifies as a mistake – cutting an apple into quarters instead of in half or forgetting to pick up your child at soccer practice?) Anyway, multiply the number of mistakes times the number of children, and, oh never mind. Forget the math - just tell yourself you're doing the best you can.

☺ Web Wit

A little boy was doing his math homework. He said to himself, "Two plus five, that son of a bitch is seven. Three plus six, that son of a bitch is nine ...."

His mother heard what he was saying and gasped, "What are you doing?"

The little boy answered, "I'm doing my math homework, Mom."

"And this is how your teacher taught you to do it?" the mother asked.

"Yes," he answered.

Infuriated, the mother asked the teacher the next day, "What are you teaching my son in math?"

The teacher replied, "Right now, we are learning addition."

The mother asked, "And are you teaching them to say two plus two, that son of a bitch is four?"

After the teacher stopped laughing, she answered, "What I taught them was, two plus two, *the sum of which*, is four."

Spicing Up Our Household

A little too much Pepper

Sometimes parents make mistakes. We may unnecessarily deny our children experiences or things because of what we fear would happen. Often these fears are unfounded, or the result is not nearly as bad as we feared.

This is not one of those times. All my worst fears about getting another dog have been realized. And then some.

In the few short months we've had our dog Pepper, I've changed diapers, wiped up countless Pepper sprays, chased her down the street in my bathrobe and fuzzy slippers (much to the amusement of the landscaping crew across the street), rescued her from a shopping trip to Eckerd Drug Store, grabbed half-eaten chipmunks out of her mouth, and cur-tailed visits to her boyfriend a few houses down.

Let's just say we have our issues. It all started immediately after we adopted her from the Atlanta Humane Society. Before we could keep her appointment to be spayed, she went into heat. My dismay at changing doggie diapers was only the teeniest bit mitigated by my pleasure in finding her a fashionable denim diaper that coordinated admirably with her dark blue collar. With two children, I'd changed thousands of diapers, but never on anything with a tail.

Our next big issue is that although she is small, she seems to have the jumping capability of an Olympic pole vaulter, and she leaps the fence in our backyard constantly. We don't think she was unhappy with her new home because she would usually run around the house and let herself in on the porch. Maybe she just liked the view from there better. That was fine by me, until a squirrel or another dog had the audacity to wander into our front yard. Then she would bust through the screens and give chase.

As a result, my front porch looks like Kansas - after the tornado. The lower screens are busted out and the lovely white wicker chairs are lying on their sides in a generally ineffective effort to keep her contained.

One of the worst times was when I drove into my driveway to see her standing in the front yard, half of a (mercifully) dead chipmunk in her mouth. My son and I convinced her to drop her treasure, which she did on the front steps. After tossing it in the bushes, I went inside to find two messages on the answering machine from a neighbor's nanny.

The first message informed me nicely that my dog was paying them a visit; the second said that she had taken the little girl's shoe when she left. My heart sank as I listened to the cries of the little girl in the background, and sank further still when I realized that my next move was to scope an entire three-mile radius searching for a tiny piece of leather.

Then there was her shopping trip. I got a call one day

from a nice man who said he found her at the shopping center up the street. The family kindly brought her home, and his wife informed me that they found Pepper trying to go in Eckerd. All we can figure is that she was perhaps concerned about her noxious doggie breath and was experimenting with minty toothpastes, or perhaps thought her coat would take on a more lustrous appearance with a new doggy shampoo.

Another day she found a joy of a different kind, when she met another black dog down the street. Because the owners weren't around during their illicit play dates, there is some dispute as to whether his name is Snickers or Elvis, but in any event, Pepper and Snickers/Elvis discovered puppy love, further motivating her daily escapes.

Then there was the inevitable conversation with my children. "You guys wanted this dog and I'm the one stuck taking care of her," I stormed one night after cleaning up after her, brushing her, and giving her food and water. That evening I was out and when I returned, my daughter had created a detailed grid, posted on the refrigerator, called "The Care and Keeping of a Pup Named Pepper!" It includes items such as "Was Pepper secured before departure? Was Pepper brushed?" I admired her effort and it warmed my heart, although it remains blank to this day.

So, as in any relationship, we're working through our issues. We're into negotiations now: if she'll do a weekly drugstore run at Eckerd and refrain from chipmunk mutilation, I'll consider a few supervised visits with Snickers/Elvis. "I'm all shook up," I said. "You're bad to the bone." She looked up at me and replied, "Don't be cruel. Just love me tender." So I'm trying to remember: she ain't nothin' but a hound dog.

Sanity Scarce
in Early Evening

I was sitting in our tiny upstairs bathroom recently, balancing a plate of warmed-up pasta on my lap while chatting with my son, who was gleefully tossing bubbles around, and listening to my daughter, who was standing in the doorway trying to emit music-like sounds from the flute. It occurred to me that this is probably not what people mean when they talk about having a family dinner. But one thing I've learned is that when there are children in the house, things do not always go according to plan. Especially during the hours between 5 and 7 p.m.

We had planned on a family dinner. Then my husband had to work late, so I fed the kids. I was eating when my son yelled from upstairs for me to come sit and talk to him while he bathed. That's when "Leave it to Beaver" turned into "Roseanne." It's not that my dinner in the bathroom was unpleasant. The conversation was good, although the ambiance was a bit lacking, and my porcelain seat was a bit hard.

Other disruptions are not so pleasant. My friend

Deborah once experienced such an occasion. Everything was on track; her daughter was bathed and in her pajamas, her son was at soccer practice, and the homework was finished. The school project was sitting on the kitchen counter drying on a newspaper. It was a green Triceratops that she and her son had spent three days planning and carefully constructing, but the time had been worth it because he was thrilled with his masterpiece.

Deborah was in her kitchen and to her horror, saw her dog, Sophie, the yellow lab, lying on the floor looking forlorn and sickly. Next to her were shreds of newspaper mixed with green chunks of regurgitated dinosaur and assorted other food products. Sophie, following her hunter instincts, had captured the Triceratops and eaten its tail, which instantly and violently disagreed with her.

Knowing that she didn't have time to make another dinosaur, Deborah briefly considered recycling the tail. However, the formerly long spiked tail had suffered somewhat during its journey through the canine digestive system, and now resembled a giant, spitball.

Remembering that her daughter had made a pink rabbit out of the same Play-Doh mixture, my friend mercilessly yanked off the bunny's leg to glue it on the dinosaur. But there was no glue in the house.

She tried to call her husband, but he was drinking champagne and eating smoked salmon at a reception in Washington, D.C. and was unreachable, for which he will pay dearly for the rest of his life. Her son returned, and Deborah threw the kids in the car and drove to the drugstore.

Confronted by a myriad of glue choices, she had to decide whether the dinosaur was constructed of porous or non-porous material. The dinosaur's outside, being baked, was non-porous, but the inside, not being completely done, was more like cookie dough. She selected some household rubber cement, and upon arriving home, successfully attached a pink bunny tail to the green Triceratops, which her son proudly took to school. He then left it on the bus on the way home.

My worst 5-7 p.m. happened when the children were small. The day had been so bad already that as a last resort I threw the kids in the bathtub in the afternoon, just so I could catch my breath. There were in there 3.2 seconds when my daughter yelled, "Christopher just pooped in the tub!" I took them out of the tub, drained it, scrubbed it and refilled it. Meanwhile the children were joyfully doing laps around the house, what we call nudie runs.

When I called them to get back in the tub, I saw that my son had continued the poop-fest, leaving deposits all over the house.

I was busy cleaning up the mess, cursing silently and wishing I knew even more bad words that I couldn't say out loud, when my husband came home. He had spoken to me a few hours earlier, heard how horrible my day had been even before the bathtub poop incident and had brought me flowers. They failed to work their magic this time. My mood was so far beyond foul, I didn't even look at them.

I went to the kitchen, poured myself a whopping glass of red wine, and retreated to the living room, congratulating myself on outwardly maintaining my composure. I wasn't even feeling guilty yet about ignoring the flowers, or thinking how unattractive I had looked, slapping around a vinegar-soaked rag, mumbling under my breath, looking like a deranged cross between Cinderella and Lady MacBeth.

I took a deep breath and started to relax, thinking that all those breathing exercises we learned during childbirth class had nothing at all to do with birthing the child, but had a lot to do with trying to raise them. Just then my daughter came in and kicked over a glass of red wine, making red Kandinsky-like patterns on my ivory rug. It is entirely possible that at that moment I actually uttered a bad word out loud.

There are two lessons here. One is that we only have so much control over the course of our lives. One minute you're calmly cooking dinner; the next you're ripping off bunny tails and contemplating the porousness of a Play-Doh dinosaur. The other lesson is that there is a reason cocktail hour starts at 5 p.m. And it has nothing to do with getting off work.

✐ Tip for School Kids
Have once-a-week room clean-ups. Ask your kids to clean up their rooms on Sunday nights and don't bug them the rest of the week. Their reward is that you will only nag them once a week about the room. If it bugs you mid-week, just close the door.

A Multilingual Family

*Men are from Mars, women are from Venus
and the kids are from Pluto*

In my household we are multilingual. We have one language spoken by the man, one by the woman, and a third by the children. And all the languages are English.

My husband and I are not unlike other couples in that we communicate differently. That means we have conversations like the following:

"What do you want for your birthday this year?"

"I don't like it when you ask me. Don't you know me well enough to figure out what I'd like?"

"But you say you don't like surprises."

"If you gave me something I wanted, that would be a surprise."

"But then you wouldn't like that!"

"After all these years together, you should know the difference between the kind of surprise I like and the kind I don't like."

The husband then goes out and buys the wife a vegetable chopper he saw being demonstrated at the mall.

He was fascinated by how quickly it turned a large zucchini into tiny uniform strips and he knows how much his wife hates to chop vegetables. He congratulates himself because with this gift, he can prove he's been paying attention to her needs.

When she opens it, starts to cry and says, "If you really loved me, you would never have bought me this!" he quickly surmises that this is not the kind of surprise she likes. Bewildered, he questions why his wife can't be more like his friend Will. Every year for his birthday, he gives Will a six-pack of St. Pauli Girl beer and he never cries when he pulls it out of the brown paper bag.

Guys have their own method of communication. My husband once talked with a friend on the phone for 20 minutes. I asked what was new. "Nothing," he says. "Oh yeah, Ed bought a new golf club – a Big Bertha. He used it last week and shot his best score ever."

Three hours later, he said, "Ed's wife had the baby yesterday." Exasperated, I asked, "Is it a boy or a girl?"

He looked at me like I was crazy. "We didn't get into the details," he said.

The key to handling a multilingual household is translation. Although my husband is still often a mystery to me, I have become adept at translating my children. Here are some examples:

Child to playmate: "You're my best friend."

Translation: You are at my house now and we both eat Fruit by the Foot the same way; by unrolling the whole thing, hanging it over our ears, putting both ends in our mouths, and trying to eat it without touching it or getting it stuck in our hair.

Child to parent: "But all the other kids watch this TV show!"

Translation: I was on the playground today and I heard Mark say that he heard that a kid in fourth grade thought he might be able to watch it when his parents go out and the baby-sitter is talking on the phone to her boyfriend.

Child: "There's never anything good to eat in the house."

Translation: Although you bought exactly what I asked for at the store, including Gushers, granola bars with M&Ms, two kinds of ice cream, and you baked chocolate chip cookies, I just saw a commercial for sprinkle-covered Ling Dings and we don't have any.

Child: "I hate school!"

This phrase actually can mean several things:

1) It's cold outside and warm in my bed.

2) They are serving those disgusting chalupas that look like dog barf for lunch.

3) My favorite sweatshirt that I always wear on Thursdays is stuffed under my bed with mustard stains on it.

4) I am never going back to school because yesterday Martha dropped green Jell-O down her shirt and I laughed so hard, milk came out of my nose and by the end of the day the kids were calling me Udder Head.

Although we speak different languages, we're working on expressing ourselves clearly and translating for the other household members when necessary. The other day my daughter was upset about something. My son, who isn't clear on the meaning of some verbs said, "Just quit bragging." Catherine said patiently, "I am not bragging. I am complaining."

And I know what I will say the next time I receive a new Dustbuster for my birthday, I'll just say truthfully, "This present really does suck."

I probably should just save myself a lot of grief and just ask him for a six-pack of Rolling Rock, invite my friend Judy over, and tell her she's my best friend because she also gets cleaning tools for her birthday and she likes to eat chocolate chip cookies with beer.

☺   Web Wit

Things I've learned From My Kids, by an anonymous mother

• If you hook a dog leash over a ceiling fan, the motor is not strong enough to rotate a 42-pound boy wearing Batman underwear and a Superman cape. It is strong enough, however, to spread paint on all four walls of a 20x20 foot room.

• If you spray hair spray on dust bunnies and run over them with rollerblades, they can ignite.

• Brake fluid mixed with Clorox makes smoke, and lots of it.

• No matter how much Jell-O you put in a swimming pool you still can't walk on water.

• The spin cycle on the washing machine does not make earthworms dizzy. It will, however, make cats dizzy. Cats throw up twice their body weight when dizzy.

• You probably do not want to know what that odor is.

• When you hear the toilet flush and the word "Uh-oh," it's already too late.

Gender Wars

They're just born that way

They say that if a group of boys came upon a strange object on the playground, they would try to destroy it. A group of girls would try to nurture it. My theory is that if it was an article of clothing, the boys would either use it for third base or tie a kid to a tree with it, while the girls would be checking to see what other colors it came in and would scope out the woods to see if they could locate some cute accessories.

I saw a program several years ago in which a series of experts expounded on the theory that boys and girls are born with similar personality traits. If the girls play with Kitty Litter Barbie and sweet little baby dolls while the boys select Rock 'em Sock 'em robots and bean each other with the frozen waffles from the play kitchen, it's only because of the way we are raising them. I thoroughly enjoyed the program and laughed myself silly. I didn't realize until the end that it wasn't a comedy special. These people had obviously never spent a day in a household where representatives of both genders were being raised.

My house is a kind of lab all its own when it comes

to gender differences. There are two children in my house, one of each flavor, who demonstrate these differences on a daily basis – "I'll be in the bathtub for a few hours," says one, as she carefully lines the bathroom counter with an enviable array of fruit and berry-scented bath products. The other one says, "Do I have to take another shower! I just took one last Wednesday," and emerges 87 seconds later, claiming to have showered, shampooed and soaped himself while miraculously remaining relatively dry, and claiming to still have some shampoo left from the bottle I bought in 1997. And while one has a delicate sneeze, and makes sure to excuse herself after each one, the other revels in any noisy emission of bodily functions, the louder the better. "But mom, if I held it in, my shoes would blow off," he says.

And then there's the whole arena of wardrobe acquisition. Rather than checking the weather forecast, my daughter monitors the possibilities of a shopping trip each morning. "We're going to the orthodontist? Do they have a gift shop there?' But mention the word "shopping" to my son and his eyes widen in terror, and he may even opt to take a shower rather than face a trip to the mall. I suppose he figures he can monitor the length of a shower himself, but a shopping trip lasts at least 287 trillion, billion hours, according to his latest calculations.

During a recent trip to Target we purchased my son's entire summer wardrobe. We located the racks of khaki shorts in the boy's department, found the most awesome pair there and grabbed three. All the same. We then determined that out of the two drawers and one shelf full of old camp, school and miscellaneous T-shirts at home, enough would still fit to last the summer. Then we select-ed two bathing suits of acceptable color and size. We were done, at least with him.

Later, much later, my son sat slumped dejectedly on the chair outside the dressing room, with his head in his heads, moaning, "I'm never going shopping with my sis-ter again!" while my daughter was delightfully in her sec-ond hour of trying on all the shorts in the department. And this was just the beginning. This was only one department, of one store.

I've learned that it is best to take the divide-and-con-quer approach, and deal with the two camps separately. My daughter and I can go clothes shopping together. With the notable exception of the polyester-bell-bot-tomed, fringe-infested Limited Too, we like the same stores. And for the next trip for my son's wardrobe, not scheduled until September, we'll leave her at home for those 20 minutes.

So are these differences something we instilled? All I know is that when my daughter was born, before we even left the hospital she declared that pink was not her color, demanded to know if diapers came in any other color and tried to schedule her first shopping trip. My son, on the other hand, enjoyed lounging in the nursery, rousing only briefly to challenge the boy baby in the adjacent bassinet to a burping contest.

The Live-In Muse

People often ask me where I get inspiration for my stories. I would love to claim to have a kindly Muse who lives in the upstairs bedroom, provides me with constant ideas, (and maybe even a little help with the housework by vacuuming every Tuesday, if I had an especially accommodating one.)

The truth is, anyone who spends a lot of time with children doesn't need a Muse. They are the constant source of inspiration. Here's a sampling of some of my conversations with my son, when he turned 10 years old.

On Taking Showers

"Christopher, don't forget to wash your hair," I yelled through the bathroom door.

"I just did."

"How could you? You've only been in there 20 seconds. Are you sure you took a shower?"

"Well, I'm kind of soggy so I think so."

"How did you take a shower so fast?" I said when my son once again supposedly completed his hygiene routine is less time than it takes me to locate the shower cap.

"I'm just speedy," he said.

"Did you even get wet?" I asked.

"Well, not very." He admitted.

On Growing Older

Once we were discussing what a good baby he was. "You were so sweet and cute when you were little," I said. "And you still are."

He nodded seriously. "Yes. All that has changed is my age and my wisdom."

A few weeks ago I took Christopher with me to the eye doctor. The technician asked him what he wanted to be when he grew up. "Older," he said.

On Pride

One morning I told Christopher he was supposed to wear a red nose for his scout troop Pack meeting the following Monday for a skit they were doing. "Are we really going to be humiliated *that* much?" he said.

Giving Advice

Last year during the hectic Christmas season, I had one of "those" days. My daughter had an afternoon tennis lesson, I had to buy the ingredients and then make fudge for teachers' presents, then get to Cub Scouts at 6:30.

Christopher then informs me that he has to wear something special for his band concert the next day at 9 a.m., but he's not sure what it is. After digging around in his school folders, he finds the notice from three weeks ago that he is supposed to wear black pants and a white shirt. He doesn't have either.

So I drop my daughter off, race through the late-afternoon traffic to Old Navy, where of course they don't have any white shirts. We do find some black pants, and although they aren't dress pants and aren't really his size, it's as close as we're going to get so we buy them anyway. I then race to pick up my daughter, then home, where I have 17 minutes to make dinner. Meanwhile we can't find his old white shirt, which I'm fairly certain is too small anyway.

Christopher strolls in the kitchen to find me standing over a pot of water that is obstinately refusing to boil, tightly clutching a fistful of spaghetti and cursing under my breath in a Grinch-like fashion about the demands on mothers during this time of year.

"If I was you I would just try to relax and enjoy the rest of my evening," he said.

On Girls

One day he said that a girl was mean to him on the bus, and bugged him when she saw him at school. His sister said, "That means she likes you."

"Why would she like me?" he asked.

I made the mistake of saying, "Because you're adorable." With that he fell on the floor, and wailed, "MOM!"

He got up and said, "Why would she be mean if she likes me?"

His father said, "Girls are like that. If she didn't like you she'd ignore you. If she teases you it means she likes you."

"Girls are so *weird*," he said.

"Boys are weird too," I said.

"Well, girls are 107% weird," he said. "Boys are just -82% weird."

On Money

"I don't waste my money on a lot of different stuff," he said once while counting up his allowance. "I just waste it on Pokemon stuff.

Peas in a Pod

Using genetics to our advantage

G enetics: the scientific study of who we can blame for our propensity to carry extra fat cells in unsightly areas, our inability to whistle a recognizable tune, and our periodic and otherwise inexplicable cravings for lime Jell-O molds with canned pears.

Genetics versus environment – it's the old debate. Which has the most influence over the emotional development of children? I like to give credit to the environment I create in the home for the good qualities and achievements, while blaming genetics, on my husband's side of the family of course, for any questionable behavior. It works out well.

That way I can take full credit if they read a lot of books (I've taken them to the library all their lives) and have good manners. (It must be the congenial atmosphere we have in the home at all times, and my southern upbringing.)

And I can blame his side of the family for any errant ways, which include chewing with their mouths open or leaving towels behind the bathroom door where they would be discovered weeks later, in a green mildewy pile. My husband actually taught me this technique. After my 1831st complaint that he doesn't listen to me, he said, "It's genetic. My dad doesn't listen to my mother either."

Recently my daughter told me she was studying genetics in school. "Oh, yeah, Mendelssohn's peas," I said, nodding knowingly.

"Mom, it's *Mendel's* peas," she said. "Mendelssohn was a German composer."

"Well, he could have had his own peas, too," I said with a huff. (Although I suppose composers are way too sophisticated to be concerning themselves with breeding plain old vegetables. If they were involved in vegetable reproduction at all, they probably worked with something more sophisticated like asparagus or the ever-intriguing artichoke.)

As part of her studies she had to conduct a genetic survey, and asked me and several of my co-workers a series of questions. I never did quite understand the point of the exercise, but it was amusing to see the pro- duction manager, the sales manager and the publisher rolling their tongues, measuring their index fingers against the length of their ring fingers and pondering over what an unattached earlobe was. I never did tell them that trying to put their foot behind their head while counting backwards from 100 was *not* part of the exper- iment – we just wanted to see how far we could push them in the name of science.

Then my daughter and I talked a little about genetics in our family. I told her that when she was little, everyone said she looked just like her daddy. "All she got from her mom was her fat thighs and sweaty feet," my husband used to joke. That is until he got tired of fixing his own dinner.

As she grew older, she looked more and more like me, and now people think we look just alike. Fortunately for her, she has several positive traits I don't have. These include her speedy metabolism, her artistic and singing ability and her organizational skills. The neatness thing appeared mysteriously one day, out of the blue, when she was about seven. She began organizing her room, making her bed, and keeping her things in order. I stared at her efforts in disbelief. Although I struggle to maintain and sometimes achieve partial order in my home, it is not a natural state, and only developed when I realized the old "lock the doors, turn out the lights, and pretend we're not here" trick wouldn't last forever. People would still show up.

As for my son, who does look just like his father, the only things he seems to have inherited from me so far are a strong dislike for any vegetables other than carrots, which I grew out of upon the discovery of Bearnaise sauce, and his impeccable sense of rhythm and superb booty-shaking skills, which I like to think I still have.

The downside to this whole theory is when the children get old enough to use it against us. I recently heard my neighbor the other day explaining her large number of car accidents, caused by her backing into people. "I get it from my mother," she said.

A Manner of Speaking

When I was growing up, saying "Yes ma'am" and "Yes Sir" was as natural as fighting with my brother and sister for the front seat every time we got in the car. It was just something we did without thinking as soon as we learned to talk. (I am really unclear *why* we always wanted the front seat, just as I'm clueless why my children fight over it to the point where they've had shouting matches in our driveway. I guess they just want to be close to me.)

But I never pushed the ma'am and sir thing with my kids and I think I regret it. I halfheartedly told my daughter to say "Yes, ma'am" to me a few years ago, to which she replied incredulously, "I don't have to say ma'am to you, you're my mother!"

I could live without the "ma'am" but what I get instead is "yeah" to everything, in spite of my constant requests of "Please say yes!" Whenever I hear "yeah," I just get images of them turning into delinquents and their future will hold "Yeah, let's go steal a car," instead of "Yes, I'd like to accept this job offer."

When I recently heard my son say "yeah" to my father, I said, "Christopher, don't say that to Grandpa. You should say, 'Yes sir, Grandpa sir!'"

To which he responded with all the apathy an 8-year-old can manage, "Whatever."

I may be losing on this particular front, but I feel pretty strongly that it's my duty to try to cram some manners into my children. I want them to behave properly and to be able to converse with all types of people with confidence. And it's important that after they spill a jar of maraschino cherry juice all over the inside of the refrigerator that they have the decency to say, "I'm sorry."

My children's school tried to aid in the effort. Last year when my daughter was in fourth grade she saw a movie about etiquette. She came home and announced she had learned to eat escargot and drink champagne at a white tie dinner.

I informed her that unfortunately we were having hamburgers and milk and she could wear a white tie if she wanted to but I hoped she wouldn't spill ketchup on it.

My guess is I'm not alone in this endeavor to teach manners, although I don't go as far as a woman I heard about who appoints a "Manners Monitor" in her household on a weekly basis. I assume their function is to inform other members when they have performed in a less-than-proper manner. As in, "Mommy, when Peter burped twice, he only said 'Excuse me' once."

So night after night I have watched my son across the dinner table, as he chews with his mouth open, his elbows on the table, complaining about the food. (Although I give him points for creativity. Last night he said he couldn't eat the quiche because it made his ears pop.)

Then what started as mild annoyance turned to abject horror when I contemplated, What if he does this at other people's houses!

Maybe it's being raised in the South, but we worry about our children's behavior and one of the highest compliments you can pay a mother is "Your children have such nice manners." I have actually heard this comment on occasion, and stop myself from responding, "Oh then he must not have tried to tie his spaghetti together to make a slingshot, and then used it to torpedo croutons across the room, like he did last night."

Then there was the time the mother said, "You know that Nerf gun Christopher brought over, the one that shoots the little yellow balls? Well he and David took turns shooting my daughter's 80-year-old piano teacher with it."

I can only hope he said "excuse me" if he made a direct hit.

A woman told me once she had taken her young son to a wedding. He was doing fine throughout the ceremony and the reception, but after a few hours he found his mom and said wearily, "Mommy, I've run out of manners."

I find this story charming and just hope I can instill enough manners in my children that they will have some out of which to run.

Sit Right Down and You'll Hear a Tale

Recently my husband and I engaged in one of our frequent intellectual exercises. We were trying to remember all the words to the theme song from "The Beverly Hillbillies."

My ever-attentive daughter listened for a few minutes, then accused us of making this song up. Incredulously I asked, "You've never seen 'The Beverly Hillbillies?'"

She looked at me disdainfully. "I've never even heard of 'The Beverly Hillbillies.'" she said.

To make matters worse, she wasn't even the least bit intrigued when I tried to explain the premise of the show, and even appeared uninterested in the entire concept of the cement pond.

Upon further inquiry, I learned the following: My kids didn't know where or even what Mayberry is, couldn't name the pig on "Green Acres" and although they had heard of "Gilligan's Island," were unable to list the name of one single character.

My husband and I looked at each other in disbelief. Where had we gone wrong? We'd been so careful to make sure they were receiving an excellent education, had been to the theater, traveled and even been to "Peter Pan on Ice." All the while, here they were, ignorant of a great expanse of American culture.

The children looked at my growing consternation in amazement. This is the mother who lectures them constantly on the rot-inducing power of TV, and admittedly has turned off such classics as "Cow and Chicken," right in the middle of a major plot development.

Meanwhile I was getting more concerned as I remembered a segment I'd heard on a radio show a few weeks before. The question the DJs posed for the listeners was this.

"What's the first thing you know?"

Callers gave answers such as, "That you're awake," or "The sound of your mother's voice."

The answer, of course is "Ol' Jed's a millionaire."

Can it be that my kids will grow up, be asked that question, and not be able to come up with a response? This could not be. It is critical that they know the answer, spend several hours pressing the redial button on their phones and not be able to get through, but be secure in their knowledge of the response.

And if not for TV theme songs from the past, how would they overcome the inevitable times of adversity ahead?

Just a few months before, I had been on our company retreat in Little St. Simon's Island. Three of us got stranded in a boat during an early morning trip through the marshland, miles from any other living human beings. Being true city folk, we had a cell phone and were able to summon a rescue party. As we sat in the swamp, with a watch out for gators and angling for position to use each other for shade, we sang the theme song from "Gilligan's Island." Except none of us could remember the opening lines, and just kept repeating, "Three-hour tour, a three-hour tour," with more and more emphasis, with the major benefit being that we scared away any hungry gators within a seven-mile radius.

When our rescue boat came, we were tempted to pump them for the missing lyric, but decided to maintain a modicum of dignity after our pathetic inability to restart the boat because we hadn't paid attention in boat class. (I've never been sure what a modicum was, but I believe it's more than a smidgen, but less than a tad.) Fortunately, when we reached the dock, we were able to obtain the information from the first two coworkers we saw, who commiserated with the seriousness of our situation.

But before I succumbed to total panic at my lack of ability to instill any meaningful culture into my children, we had finally found common ground with "The Brady Bunch." We had a quite a lively discussion about which brother is the cutest and what exactly did Mrs. Brady do all the time if Alice did the shopping, cooking and housework? After we all sang a rousing rendition of the theme song together, I felt much better. And tomorrow I'm making flash cards – with the names of all the characters on "Gilligan's Island."

Culinary Crises

Or why moms and entertaining don't mix

I knew that my culinary skills declined somewhat in the past few years. But a recent event forced me to examine the depths to which they had fallen. I burned Rice Krispie Treats.

If there were a list of 10 things you can make in the kitchen that can't be messed up, Rice Krispie Treats would be on it, right after a peanut butter sandwich. So how did this happen, you ask? Many people did. Including my children, over and over.

Without going into too many details, it has to do with severe short-term memory loss. I simply forgot the marshmallows and butter were on the stove. When I went back to the kitchen, I found a bubbling vat of brownish-white slime. It looked like primordial ooze from which the Pillsbury Dough Boy would emerge. I briefly entertained the notion that although the treats had cooked approximately 187 times longer than they should have, they would still be okay. Then I tasted them. Imagine what a piece of melted tire mixed with a gooey coat of burst sugar frosting with the consistency or road tar would taste like. That would be better.

So my cooking skills have definitely degenerated. But

that isn't the only reason I don't really entertain much anymore, beyond family dinners and the occasional cook-out. I blame it on the arrival of children. And I don't think I'm alone. There are other women, whose entertaining, if it hasn't ceased completely, has deteriorated from Chicken Wellington with Currant Sauce to Pigs in a Blanket with Yellow Mustard.

Here are two reasons why:

1) Although we can still maintain control over the meal, with the addition of children to a household, there are many uncontrollable factors that can severely damage the atmosphere of a party.

I heard the story of a woman who was having a dinner party. She left some butter out to soften and her four-year-old seized the opportunity to practice her spreading skills. On the cat.

Then she cut all the cat's whiskers off, so that the cat lost her sense of space. Greased and whiskerless, Pinstripe streaked through the dining room, and bounced around every available surface, leaving a trail of grease spots on rugs, chairs, and any other surface her lard-laden coat touched.

One year, we planned to have Easter Brunch on our front porch. As were setting the table, my son, who was in the midst of potty training, decided it was a good time to climb on top of the table and practice his aim, all over the newly starched and ironed white tablecloth. I didn't have another tablecloth, so we improvised. Although it was a sheet, I thought the scenes of Winnie-the-Pooh and friends frolicking in the 100-acre wood were a nice touch for spring.

2) Although the kitchen may be well stocked, finding the tools and ingredients when we need them is a crapshoot.

For example, my children once peeled off all the labels on my canned goods. At the time, the inside of the Spaghetti-Os label had a temporary tattoo, so it stood to reason that perhaps the label of the artichoke hearts might reveal something equally fun. I was trying to make lasagna and didn't know whether I was opening a can of diced tomatoes or fruit cocktail. From experience, I can assure you that the two are not interchangeable.

Another time I was making brownies and got out my measuring cups to measure oil. I noticed that it seemed to be coming out just as fast as I was putting it in, causing an oil slick reminiscent of the Exxon Valdez on my kitchen floor. Yes, there was a hole in the bottom of the cup. My daughter had gone through a phase of fascination with the power of the microwave to melt plastic. For months I found spoons that were twisted into pretzel shapes, plastic cups in unidentifiable geometric forms, and even a McDonald's miniature Barbie toy flattened to the point that Barbie's chest actually approximated the scale of a normal human being.

Or you may find that the flour is all gone, victim to a papier mache project gone astray, the baking soda box is empty because the children dumped it on the dog after reading on the box that it kills odors. And the mixing bowls are in the basement, filled with hardened papier-mache.

I've decided to do something about my culinary downfall. I've bought new measuring cups, metal this time, pulled out my old copies of Gourmet, and I'm planning my next dinner party. The invitation list is completely cat- and children-free and instead of Rice Krispie Treats, I'm having a no-cook treat for dessert: berries and ice cream. Now I just need to dig my ice cream scoop out of the sandbox.

Four

Celebrations and Vacations

Endless Summer

When I was a child, a day in the summer flew by at roughly 8 1/2 times the speed of a day in February – a swirl of swimming, eating popsicles, playing Kick the Can and sitting in our homemade hammocks reading books. One of the biggest shocks of growing up and getting a job is that they actually expect you to work all summer, with one day off to eat watermelon on the fourth of July.

But I figured when I had children my summers would again be fun-filled and would fly by. We'd relax by the pool, read books in the afternoon and have leisurely summer dinners of grilled chicken and delicious pasta salad I made, following recipes from the magazines I'd read while they took naps.

After spending several summers at home with children I know that the longest day of the year is definitely in summer, and the only time that flies by is the time they are asleep. In fact, I've had some days where Superman must have turned back the earth, because they were at least 87 hours long.

The reality of a summer day with two preschoolers goes something like this:

Morning:

Wake up to howling, dirty baby. Change diapers and clothes. Make breakfast. Clean up breakfast. Change more diapers. Ask older child to clean up spilled grape juice, neglecting to tell her not to use your new white T-shirt. Promise older child you will go to pool today. Put baby down for nap. Take four-minute shower with door open to hear older child answer phone and say, "She can't come to the phone. She's naked." Get baby up. Rewash clothes you forgot about that are still in washing machine from two days ago. Make lunch. Clean up lunch.

Afternoon:

Help older child find a clean bathing suit and the Barbie towel because she had decided she is too mature for the Barney towel she begged you for last week. Put baby down for afternoon nap and try to read books to older child who is whining to go swimming and detailing all the disadvantages of having a baby in the house, one of which is "He thinks he is the boss of the house." Get baby up. Find older child who has run out to the front yard and turned on the sprinkler, soaking the inside of your car, the rugs on the front porch and trampled your newly-planted flowers. Put baby in swim diaper. Put on bathing suit and after quick glance in the mirror tell yourself it's just the lighting that seems to make the pregnancy stretch marks so visible. Drive to pool. Put baby in shade and chase preschooler around pool.

Evening:

Make Kraft macaroni and cheese for dinner, adding a little bit of your own grated cheese to assuage guilt over dinner out of a box. Clean up. Bathe children. Put to bed. Get mail out of mailbox from last three days and add new magazines to large pile of unread material, including the Christmas issue of Southern Living and the letter from college roommate, which you put down after reading the first line - "It must be like one long vacation to stay home with your kids."

Next day. Repeat.

One year I had signed my children up for a few Bible schools, which are a wonderful thing for mothers of young children. Admittedly, the religious aspect may be secondary. As I heard one weary mother say during registration, "If there was a Hindu Bible School, I'd sign up for that too." The next year they decided they didn't want to sign up for anything. The whole summer. Idiotically, I agreed. But they did agree to go to our church's Bible School, so I was excited that I'd would have approximately 12 1/2 hours of freedom during the summer.

But I sent in my form late. When I called to make sure they had received the form, the church lady said, "I see you signed up for snacks. I need someone to coordinate those, and be here every day. Can you do that?"

"Sure," I said, not being able to think of an acceptable alternative to "I'm trying to get away from my kids, not provide snacks for hundreds of others."

I never turned in a form late again.

Life changes though. Last weekend I was at our pool, sitting in a lounge chair, happily reading about eyebrow waxing in Vogue while my kids, now 8 and 11, swam. At least three mothers of preschoolers made envious comments while chasing their children around.

"I've heard a few Bible Schools still have openings," I said.

✎ Travel Tip

When you're on a long car trip and the kids are fussing, have the person in the passenger seat keep a loaded water gun. If the fussing gets out of hand, just reach over and give them a squirt. I haven't personally tried this because I just thought of it, so if you try it, let me know how it goes.

☺ Web Wit

Kids respond to our questions:

How can a stranger tell if two people are married?
You might have to guess, based on whether they seem to be yelling at the same kids.

What do you think your mom and dad have in common?
Both don't want any more kids.

Why did God make mothers?
She's the only one who knows where the scotch tape is.

Is anything about your mom perfect?
Just her children.

What would it take to make your mom perfect?
On the inside she's already perfect. Outside, I think some kind of plastic surgery.

Why did God give you your mother and not some other mom?
God knew she likes me a lot more than other people's moms do.

Road Rules

Tossing everyday limits out the window
key to surviving car trips

My husband asked me several years ago when we would be driving to St. Louis again to see his family. "I'd rather stick hot pins in my eyes and be slowly consumed by flames than travel that far in a car with children again," I said.

My kids are great, and I don't generally don't mind riding in a car. But somehow the combination of children plus lengthy car trip equals one of my ideas of hell. (The other is owning a bed and breakfast, but that's another story.)

We had made the 21-hour round trip several times. I would sit wedged into a tiny space in the front seat, surrounded by bags of toys, snacks and magazines I'd rarely get to read, with barely enough room to wriggle my toes. The kids would alternate complaining about the behavior of each other, "She's looking at me funny again," or "His big toe is close to invading MY side," with requests to play the Raffi tape for the 187th time.

Meanwhile my husband is barreling down the highway at about 107 miles per hour. While I appreciated the fact we might arrive at our destination sooner, I was more concerned with arriving with all body parts intact. But any gentle reminders on my part always drew the same response. "It only looks like I'm speeding from your angle. I'm really only going 65," he would say, despite the fact that we routinely missed exits signs because all the words were a blur, and we once made it through the entire state of Kentucky in 37 and a half minutes.

If I felt comfortable enough to pull out a magazine, I would have to turn my back to the door, and hold it up high to look at it, because otherwise my husband would lean over and stare at the ads of the semi-clad women, endangering the lives of his entire family for a glimpse at shapely buttocks in a lime green thong.

On one return trip I reached my limit. It was raining, we had been in the car for eight hours, and were going over Mont Eagle in Tennessee, a harrowing experience in good weather with a cautious driver. My mental state was such that I seriously begged my husband to let me out of the car on the side of the road. After a heated discussion about why this was not a good idea, (and in retrospect I suppose I would agree), I pouted all the rest of the way to Atlanta.

But then we learned the secret to a smooth ride is based on the principle of the inversion of everyday limits at home. Simply put, the more junk food and TV, the happier we will all be.

I learned about the power and the glory of junk food from a guy named David, who traveled to Atlanta from Baltimore with his family to see a mutual friend of ours.

I was at the house when he pulled up. After the wife and kids got out I glanced in the car. It looked as if the pork rind aisle of the 7/11 had exploded in there - Skittles wrappers, Chips Ahoy crumbs, smashed Cracker Jacks, lollipops welded to seat covers. You name it, his upholstery was wearing it. He shrugged his shoulders. "It keeps them happy," he said.

After assuring myself that all those years of careful nutrition might not necessarily be blown by one day of wanton intake of Slim Jims, I've followed that philosophy as well. Before every car trip we make a stop at the drug store and I let my kids go crazy. The only stipulations are: 1) all things chocolate must be shared with me and 2) I get my own box of Bugles, which I eat off my fingers.

But by far the best thing we ever did was invest in a portable TV/VCR. Plug that baby in, and the children are occupied for hours. Although they may miss minor sites of interest, such as the Mississippi River and the lakes of Kentucky, they can recite every line of "Toy Story" after watching it five times in a row. And with the use of two sets of headphones, the grown-ups no longer have to endure the twangy notes and confusing lyrics of "I'm My Own Grandpa." So we are able to ride along in blissful silence, with only an occasional request for another Frosted Pop Tart. And I'm able to look at magazines to my heart's content, but for safety's sake, I read The New Yorker in the car and save Vogue for when we're on firm ground.

On the Fantasy Road Again

I've never really cared about cars. Even in high school I didn't care what guys drove, and even dated a guy for a year whose heater in his green Cougar never worked. (We were late to a movie one time when the inside of his windshield was covered with ice.) I drove my first car, a Volkswagen Rabbit, for 11 years and finally got rid of it when the hatchback broke and I had to hold it open with my head when I was loading anything in the back.

But I do like for a car to get me from Point A to Point B. For about the past year my 10-year-old car has taken to getting me from Point A to Point A 1/2 or point A and 3/4. "The Deathtrap" – as I affectionately began referring to it when my windshield wiper quit when I was driving on the highway in the rain, after we just got it fixed for stalling while I was driving on the highway – is on its last wheels.

I need a new car.

While idly flipping through the classifieds, on the way to the station wagon section, the Miata section leapt off the page. You know those cute little adorable convertibles, the kind that can hold one sack of groceries, but only if you don't fill it all the way to the top. The kind that holds one other person, if you don't have a sack of groceries. The kind that no mother of two children who drives carpools should allow herself to even consider. I doubt the windshield is even big enough to fit a carpool number over one digit.

Yet I began to picture myself in a Miata. My fantasy became quite detailed, as the best ones always are. I saw myself tooling around town, down Northside Drive to be exact, on a beautiful day, sunny and 75 degrees. The top is down, of course, and my CD player is full of grown-up CDs with songs that don't rhyme and may even contain an occasional bad word - maybe I'm shifting gears to the Indigo Girls "Shame on You." I've got my way-cool designer sunglasses on. I'm wearing a new outfit with a sleeveless top for maximum sun exposure, from the one day I actually went shopping for myself rather than my children.

As an added bonus, I fantasize about a handsome man, probably with an Italian accent, slowing down and looking at me. And he doesn't see a harried mom with Cheerios stuck to her cheek from leaning over to pry a school report out from under the seat, car piled with old clothes to give to charity, two kids punching each other in the back seat. He doesn't hear Star 94 blaring that Cher song again, (the soundtrack of my daughter's life). He sees a cool, calm, collected woman, whose hair even looks gorgeous in a convertible. (Hey, it's my fantasy and my hair can look good if I want it to.)

But here the fantasy comes to an abrupt halt. Where could I possibly be going? I couldn't fit all the overdue library books in that car, no way the bedding plants for my yard would go in the trunk, and the big display boards I need to buy for my son's science project wouldn't have a prayer. Not to mention what to do with that extra kid.

So for now I'm still driving the station wagon, with its school stickers on the bumper, the pale ghosts of carpool numbers past on its windshield, and the big gash in the side where my neighbor dropped a metal awning on it. And yes, it has its share of Fruit Roll-up wrappers, crushed Lucky Charms and Happy Meal toys scattered inside. And it may break down on occasion, but it holds a week's worth of groceries, several bales of pine straw, any size science project and even a couple of bicycles. I can pick up six Cub Scouts whenever I need to, or transport a whole slew of girls to a slumber party, sleeping bags and stuffed animals included.

But I console myself with a contingency fantasy. Maybe the next time my car breaks down, that handsome Italian guy will stop to rescue me. And he'll be driving a Miata.

🖊 Travel Tip

Pack a road trip kit for each child containing several small toys or treats. Let them open one for each 50 or 100 miles. If this plan only increases the number of "How much further" cries you have to hear, tell them they have to skip a turn if they ask that question!

Dancing Mice, Gorilla Make for Cheesy Evening

They say you always remember your first time. I remember everything about it – the lights, the mood, the ambiance, the music, the food, the drumming gorilla robot. My first trip to Chuck E. Cheese,

We headed out in a driving rainstorm with another family, all packed into my station wagon. The two girls, both two years old, were in the third seat, singing happily. I think the whole thing was even my idea. I thought it would be a good way to go out with friends and not have to go through the torturous effort and expense of finding a baby sitter.

I walked innocently into the brightly colored building, which was lit up like a Las Vegas casino. I don't know if it was the music, the lights, or the piercing screams of the clientele that I noticed first, but the combination struck me with an overwhelming force. I started laughing, then stopped abruptly as a feeling of monumental horror enveloped me.

It was a Defining Moment. One of those moments you

never forget, generally because it accompanies some profound realization about your life. Like the first time you get sick in college. It really hits you that you are on your own. There is no one to wheel a television in your room and make you strawberry malts and grilled cheese sandwiches. All you have now is an apathetic roommate, who responds when you say you don't feel good, "Well, if you throw up, do it on your side of the room."

I was having such a moment at Chuck E. Cheese. It was a Friday night. We weren't putting our name on a list at a trendy intown restaurant. We weren't waiting in line to see the latest movie. We weren't attending the theatre, or even a cocktail party. We were at Chuck E. Cheese. And we belonged there.

After adjusting to the noise level, I took a look around. It looked like one of those bacteria-laden slides you view under a microscope; only these were children running around in mass chaos. There were parents running, too. I saw one father, jogging with knees bent low to the ground in an effort to keep his beer from spilling, chasing a toddler who was gleefully doing laps around the salad bar, occasionally grabbing a pack of crackers and stomping on them.

As our children ran off, shrieking with joy, we figured out the system. You had to have gold tokens to go on miniature rides – a plane, a helicopter, a racecar, and a merry-go-round. Each token cost a quarter. We bought five dollars worth, plenty for the entire evening. Three minutes later, our daughter begged for more. We let the kids ride for a few minutes, racking up $87 in tokens, and ordered a pizza and sat down. We were just about to start an adult conversation when our friend's child stood up in the booth. She was in the process of potty training, but this time she missed the train. We had to move.

After the pizza came and I cut my daughter's slice into 137 child-sized fragments, I tried to talk to my friends again. No such luck. It was time for The Show. Singing bears, dancing mice and a drumming gorilla, all at a noise level to rival that of a tractor-pull. Conversation was not an option. I grabbed the pitcher and poured myself another beer.

As we drove home, the kids wired and the adults exhausted, I realized that between chasing children, locating tokens, and listening to "You Say Happy, I Say Birthday," sung repeatedly, we never had a chance to talk with our friends. We found out that one friend had lost his job because of company relocation only when his daughter sang, "My daddy was fired, my daddy was fired," all the way home.

I never went back to Chuck E. Cheese willingly and never on a weekend night. My children have been invited to parties there, but if I am crafty enough I can manage to get them rides both ways. Once, in total desperation, I offered to cook dinner for a month for one mother if she would go in my place. She upped it to two months and I had to pass.

Another particularly traumatic experience occurred when I took my daughter to a birthday party there and stayed to hang around with my son, who was about two at the time. I put him in a high chair to eat pizza and enjoy the wildly entertaining Dancing Bears and Drumming Gorillas, who must have an open-ended gig there. When it was over, we could not remove him from the high chair. I tried every which way, but he was most definitely stuck. He started crying, and we finally called over a manager over, who assisted us in extracting my son from the seat, and also gave him a balloon. As I was thanking the manager, my son, mighty grateful to be free at last, ran over to where the rides were. I followed him approximately 15 seconds later. He was nowhere to be found.

I searched desperately for my little boy, knowing logically that he couldn't have gotten far, but the fear and panic rising to the point where I was about to start screaming, with no small amount of hysteria. Just then, a little blond curly head popped out of bottom of the ball pit. He had been lying there, covered by 87 million plastic balls, oblivious to the sound of his mother's screeching voice.

My biggest coup was when my daughter was invited to another birthday party there and my husband had to take her because I was having a day of beauty at Spa Sydell. Right when I was having my soothing, stress-reducing massage, he was searching for our daughter at the bottom of a germ-infested ball pit.

The weekend after that first trip to Chuck E. Cheese, we hired a baby-sitter and went out to a popular new restaurant. Our of our (childless) friends complained about the lengthy wait. I said, "I've got a glass of wine, I only have to cut up my own food, and there are no cracker-stomping toddlers or drum-beating gorillas in sight. I am in heaven."

And I was.

Sensuous Squids, Dancing Krystal Burgers and a Moon Pie

Adventures on a Brownie camp-out

The Girl Scout motto is: Be Prepared. Unless I had been the captain of Noah's Ark I am not really sure how I could have prepared for my recent adventure with my daughter as she experienced that most sacred of rituals for a young American girl – the brownie camp-out.

(Some may argue that ours was not a true camp out and given the fact that we stayed in cabins, ate every meal out and didn't even drive by a latrine, they may be right. But we had our tough moments. The coffee I got at McDonald's in the morning was not up to its usual law-suit-inducing temperature and the cornbread at Cracker Barrel was not as sweet as I like it. But we managed.)

That year marked the 85th anniversary of the Girl Scouts. So Troop 3685 celebrated in the only manner appropriate, by joining a parade of brown and green clad scouts from all over the Southeast in an event called Bridgefest, which consisted of marching across the pedestrian bridge in Chattanooga while dancing and singing to "YMCA" and posing with a mascot dressed as a Krystal hamburger, then enjoying a Surge Cola and a Moon Pie in a tent near the Tennessee Aquarium as a man dressed as a fish hovered nearby twitching his gills.

We started our camp out on Friday afternoon. The four girls assigned to me amused themselves during the drive by making up stories, their content a combination of "E.T." meets "Little House on the Prairie," mixed in with "Goosebumps." We knew we had arrived at our destination when we saw Yogi Bear waving at us from I-75. The Jellystone Campground is basically a trailer park with a few cabins. As we stopped to check in, one of the leaders said, "Hey Jan, I just heard there is a tornado warning." My mind raced: Tornado. Trailer Park. Knowing the ability of one to attract the other, it did not take me long to realize that this was not a good situation.

The cabins were nice and we even had electricity, although if we hadn't we could have still seen from the lights of the cars passing on 1-75, which was approximately 87 feet behind us. After getting settled, which involved the girls opening up their bags, throwing everything on the floor, climbing in their bunks and shrieking until I chased all the bugs out with a broom, we headed out for pizza, then to an IMAX movie in downtown Chattanooga.

The movie was about ocean life, and was in 3-D. It was way cool. We got to wear big plastic glasses and the girls waved their arms in front of them, trying to grab the fish that looked like they were swimming right at us. Fortunately they didn't ask any questions about the squid orgy that was portrayed so vividly.

When we came out of the theater, we met the deluge. The worst thunderstorm I had ever experienced. I drove back on an unfamiliar highway, that was undergoing construction, with five brownies, one brownie leader and one windshield wiper that decided at that point to quit. While trying to chat casually with the leader, I was really saying a combination of the Our Father and the Girl Scout promise, which went something like this: "Our Father, who art in heaven, get me out of this storm and on my honor I will try to do my best to do anything you want, especially for those at home, even if that includes being the Bible School snack coordinator again."

When we finally made it back, I sent the girls into the cabin to grab their toothbrushes, and we drove through the field that had become a swamp, to go to the bathroom. (See, we *were* roughing it.)

After a night of thunderstorms, worthy in their intensity of the midnight storm scene in "King Lear" we awoke to a gray but dry day, and my car had sunk only halfway into the mud. We drove into Chattanooga for Bridgefest and afterwards the troops gathered for refreshments and an Olympic-style pin-trading frenzy. Scouts had taken scraps of pipe cleaners, felt, yarn and other materials and transformed them into totally awesome pins such as milk shakes, campfires, ladybugs and caterpillars. My favorite was the S'More, with felt for the chocolate and graham cracker and a cotton ball for the marshmallow, made by Troop 345 from Fairdale, KY.

So maybe our camp out was a little different from the ones I experienced as a child: no sailor hats dropped down latrines, no bears eating our food and no night so cold that my mother wrapped my sleeping bag in plastic wrap in a futile attempt to keep me warm so that I felt like a giant refrigerated leftover. But I did experience the joy of the simple pleasures in life: given the tornado forecast, the simple gratitude of waking up in the same spot on the earth where I went to sleep; the warm feeling we got each time we passed by the smiling figure of Yogi Bear, his plastic arm raised in a permanent wave; and that special rush that you can only achieve from the combination of a Surge Cola and a Moon Pie.

◮ Comments from Campers

These are from students at my kids' school after returning from an overnight expedition.

I didn't really understand how taking a shower could ruin the whole experience. It would have been a lot better with running water.

Being dirty for four straight days taught me how lucky I am to live in a society where I can take a shower.

I learned how to go to the bathroom in the woods and not get any on myself.

I found that I could go without make-up for a couple of days and live.

I especially disliked the random appearance of unidentified flying hamburgers in my tent.

The food was terrible, the outhouses stunk, and the rain made everything miserable, but I really enjoyed the whole expedition.

Star Surfing

The no-cook, no-latrine, no-fishing anti-camp-out

My first camp-out with my daughter's Girl Scout troop was quite an adventure, involving a tornado in a trailer park, an IMAX movie with actively reproducing squids on the screen, dancing giant hamburgers and an entire troop juiced up on Surge soda and honey buns for the long car ride home.

Although lacking in dancing meat products of any kind, our most recent camp-out proved just as adventurous.

Our troop set off in the late Friday afternoon traffic towards Mentone, Ala., my station wagon trailing the other two vans in a quasi-caravan. Less than 15 minutes away from our camp, I saw the two vans pulled over and the flashing lights of a police car. After a heart-stopping 45 seconds, we learned that a tractor-trailer had overturned on the road to our camp, blocking the mountain road and necessitating a 90-minute detour. But being the well-prepared scouts that we were, we were able to easily adjust: We called the restaurant and changed our reservation for dinner.

After finding the camp and dropping off our gear in our spacious multi-roomed cabin, we headed to a lovely restaurant with a mountain view and had a delicious steak dinner. Afterward we met Chad, our guide, who took us on a midnight hike.

Chad, who the girls decided to call Ron for reasons unknown, proved an able guide, and led us down to the river where he told us stories about the stars. He then led us back to the field where he introduced us to the concept of star surfing. Star surfing is where you look up, pick out a star to focus on, then twirl round and round really fast, then stop in surfer position, trying to maintain your balance and the contents of your stomach. It truly does feel like you're surfing, or at least how I imagine how it feels because I'm generally horizontal on a float when I'm in the ocean, saving the vertical position for dry land.

For me, the night was rather uneventful. When one of the star surfers got sick, her bunkmates found the grown-ups in the other room to deal with it. I got the report the next morning. They knocked on the door of the room and asked if there were any adults there, and one sleepy mother quickly replied "No." It didn't work.

The next day Chad/Ron led us in the first activity: "Makeshift Mansions." We climbed up a hill and Chad/Ron divided the girls into four teams, gave them a bag with plastic tarps and other items and instructed them to make a shelter in the woods. Accustomed only to coed groups, he was a little surprised at the results. These girls' shelters included kitchens, hot tubs, walk-in closets and family rooms, all of which we got to see on the first-ever "Makeshift Mansion Tour of Homes."

After an activity on the low ropes course, which involved the girls trying to swing on a rope to safety over a field of poisonous peanut butter, we headed to our last activity – Feed Your Face. No, it wasn't a feeding frenzy, but rather a facial done with natural products. Ron/Chad explained the concept of natural exfoliation as he gallantly spread a mixture of oatmeal and honey all over his bearded face. We enthusiastically (and rather messily) followed suit. Next, we divided into groups of four, and he passed around several types of herbs, which we could select and throw in our large plastic salad bowl. He poured steaming water in the bowl, and the four of us moms leaned over, with a sheet covering our heads to hold in the steam, looking like giant mushrooms.

All in all, it was my kind of camp-out – steak dinners, plenty of sleep in my own room with an adjoining bath-room, and a facial. For our next "camp-out" I've heard we're checking out a bed-and-breakfast in Charleston. Anybody know any good steak restaurants and spas there?

✐ Camp-out Tips: Food

Large ice blocks in your cooler last much longer than either ice cubes or freezer packs. Make your own ice block by filling a plastic milk container with water and placing in your freezer. A large block made in this way can last up to four to five days in your cooler.

Boil extra water at mealtime and keep it in a Thermos so you can make a hot beverage between meals or at bedtime without hav-ing to heat up your camp stove again.

Halloween Costumes
for Every Stage of Life

I consider myself somewhat of an expert on the subject of Halloween costumes. I have sewn more costumes than Seattle has coffee beans, hosted numerous grown-up Halloween parties, attended several children's costume parades, and watched "It's the Great Pumpkin, Charlie Brown!" at least 37 times. As the self-proclaimed Queen of Halloween, I have observed the stages of life through the evolution of the costume a person adorns for Halloween.

Infancy: The infant demonstrates little resistance to any embarrassing costume the parents wish to put on him or her. This is a big time for little lambs, peas in a pod, baby cows and little pumpkins. It has not been determined whether infants have any idea of the silliness bestowed upon them, or just lack the necessary physical skills to rescue their dignity. There is a big increase in the sale of Super Glue during October as parents attempt to attach antlers, pig ears and foliage to the bald heads of babies.

I did it too. I dressed my daughter up in a clown costume and took her to a few neighbors' houses. She did look cute, but more important, I got to eat the candy.

Toddlers: These are the prime years for adorable costumes. I have no scientific evidence to support this; however, I have a theory that one of the reasons mothers go through the physical discomforts of pregnancy and childbirth, not to mention the financial and emotional investment of raising children, is to see them in their Halloween costumes when they are toddlers. There is nothing cuter than a three-year-old dressed as a ladybug, a lion or practically anything from the mammal family. Older preschoolers may be firefighters, ballerinas, princesses and cowboys. The popular Disney character of the year is sure to have many followers. Many parents were relieved by the popularity of Pocahontas, a much easier costume to assemble than the Little Mermaid.

Elementary school: Girls may still dress as princesses or ballet dancers, and animals are still popular. A boy this age wouldn't be caught dead as a furry animal or anything cute. Super heroes are big. Anything with a bloody or severed limb, blown-off face, visible bodily fluid or with an alien exploding from the chest is considered attractive.

Although discussions about costumes for Halloween may begin somewhere around Valentine's Day, the wise parent waits until October before making any investment in time or materials. Many a child has declared a passionate wish for say, a Power Ranger costume, only to declare on Oct. 30, an even more passionate desire to be a tube of toothpaste.

The teenage years: Trick-or-treating becomes optional, but in any event, parents are out of the picture. The male teenager, who has been known to eat the equivalent of a Volkswagen in food at one sitting, is intrigued enough by the possibility of free candy to temporarily forget about being cool. He will pull himself away from "Southpark" long enough to grab one of Mom's designer pillowcases, and maybe draw on a scar or don an eye patch or some other half-baked attempt at a costume. Then he will proceed to the neighbor's houses and in a deep voice far past the early stages of puberty, hold out his pillowcase and grunt something like "Unnh."

Meanwhile, teenage girls gather in a friend's home, giggle about how juvenile trick-or-treating is, and compare the number of fat grams in a Milky Way versus a Snickers.

College: Many adult themes now emerge, often involving an empty cardboard box being placed on one's head or prophylactics on heretofore unsheathed areas. Girls who are novices come up with clever ideas, like a refrigerator or a garbage bag full of leaves. Girls with more experience know that boys will actually talk to them if they wear lots of make-up and the shortest skirt possible.

Adulthood: Grown-ups who have taken on the awesome responsibilities of life often look at dressing up for Halloween as a release. They take this opportunity to live out fantasies, sometimes with shocking results. One such costume I saw was Miss America. Not too unusual until you realize this was years ago when Vanessa Williams was Miss America, and this costume consisted of a beige body stocking, a crown, and the artful use of colorful markers. Another woman was covered in blown-up balloons. Men spent all evening trying to get close to her, especially the ones with sharp edges to their costumes.

As for me, one year I was Fabio. I had black boots, black leggings, a five o-clock shadow drawn on with dark concealer, and a flowing silk shirt, opened to bare my large plastic masculine chest. Talk about fantasies. It was the first time in my life that men stared at my chest all night.

☠ Halloween Tips

You want to be prepared early but are concerned about your ability to stay away from the seven bags of yummy chocolate treats you bought for Halloween? And we all know that hide-it-from-yourself trick never works. Do what I do – only buy candy that you don't really like.

Don't bother with cooking a real dinner on Halloween. The kids are too excited to eat it anyway. My two favorites are chili, which is easy to eat in between answering the door, or pizza, which is always good for breakfast the next day.

Watch your pets around the treats! Chocolate contains theobromine, which can be toxic for dogs and cats.

Costumes don't have to be store-bought or expensive. Some of the best ones are thrown together from items you have around the house. I used to love to sew my kids' costumes, but don't start too early. I saw one mother in the fabric store who had slaved over a princess costume, only to be informed a week before Halloween that her darling wanted to be a hot dog instead!

The Night Watch

Surviving the spend-the-night party

I've learned to use the words "never" and "always" sparingly. I've had to backtrack too many times. As in, I will *never* stuff marshmallows in my children's mouths to keep them quiet for a minute so I can finish a phone call. I will *always* watch what I say in front of them and *never* call the evil person who almost rammed into me on the street a deservedly bad name.

But I felt pretty comfortable with my statement that I would never host a spend-the-night birthday party. I'm still catching up on all those sleepless nights from when they were babies. And if I wanted to stay up all night and listen to giggling and stomping around, I would just move back to my old college apartment where the neighbors were notorious for their late-night shenanigans.

We've always had birthday parties at home and they only lasted 1 1/2 hours. Granted, they were labor intensive. It was generally the crafts that sounded so cute that got me into trouble. For example:

• For the "Dress Up Your Teddy Bear Tea Party" I sewed dozens of ballerina skirts for all sizes of teddy bears out of pink netting and binding tape. It was worth it, because the teddy bears all seemed to really enjoy dressing up, except for the big brown one who said the skirt made her hips look fat.

- For the Train Party I cut pictures of choo-choo trains out of napkins and glued them to small white painters' caps. To further complement the theme, I enlisted my husband's help to make a train cake. (Those were the days when I said I would *never* serve a store-bought cake. I've since discovered the joys of the Publix bakery.) We called that cake "The Little Engine That Could." More like the little cake that could, and did take five hours, three tubs of frosting and seven bottles of food coloring to make.

- For the Star Wars party I painted a huge green blob-like creature onto a white sheet, severely testing the limits of my artistic talent. I then drew black circles onto orange Ping-Pong balls and put duct tape on the back of them for a game of "Pin-the-Eyeball-on-the-Alien."

- I found tiny sombreros and drew colored rings around the brims, made enough yarn braids for the puppets' hair to reach from here to Chattanooga and glued buttons onto socks for the one-and-only Mexican Sock Puppet Party.

- For the Batman Big Wheel Party, I made 14 batman capes. They looked awesome and the kids loved them, but some of the super heroes cried when the ends got stuck in the pedals of their Big Wheels.

We've also hung up our share of piñatas, which are made of the most impenetrable material known to man. I've yet to see a child actually break one, despite hours of whacking. We usually ended up cutting ours open with the cake knife, or in one memorable episode, actually lighting one with the matches meant for the birthday candles and setting the whole thing on fire, turning the candy inside into flying, smoldering bits of melted plastic. If cars were made out of piñata material we could go around bumping into each other at will with no dents, no damage and the highways would be much more festive places to be.

But I enjoyed doing all these things, and if I got a little harried during the party, I could at least look at the children as they finger painted with blue icing on my new drapes and say "Well, at least they're going home soon."

Not this year. Somehow we ended up hosting not one, but two spend-the-night parties. Two nights in a row. I'm not sure how it happened, but I believe it was just plain weariness induced by party negotiations that were lengthier and more emotional than the Delta pilots' negotiations. The problem could be traced back to having these children in the first place, and then being careless enough to have them both be born at the end of summer.

Our preparations for the two-night marathon included pulling all the furniture out of our family room, after we remembered that we didn't have a basement, and purchasing enough doughnuts for a meeting of the Fraternal Order of Police.

The first night was for the boys. Eight of them, ages 6 and 7. The agenda was Pool, Pizza, Chocolate Chip Cookie Cake and Rainbow Ice Cream, Presents, Bingo, Movie, Bed.

It all went surprisingly well, and I was asleep by 10 p.m. I even felt slightly guilty when my friend Terri brought me a cup of coffee and a muffin from Starbucks to help compensate for what she had anticipated would be a frolic-filled and sleepless night.

Girls' night came next. Nine, girls, age 9 and 10. The agenda was exactly the same, but was altered slightly when one of the presents was a CD by Hanson, the teen idols of whom I was completely unaware. (Note to diary: this is the day I realized I am officially Out of It with the preteen set.) So we had a dance contest. The winner got an extra box of Nerds.

I'll admit I was a little shocked to see some of the dance moves these 9-year-old girls had acquired. I thought they weren't supposed to know about bumping and thrusting until they had at least were old enough to watch cable TV when their parents weren't home. One mother told me later that her daughter was learning such things from the new au pair, not a good situation, in my opinion.

The girls stayed up later because they hadn't got the required number of hours of giggling in, but by 9 a.m. the next day, it was all over. We not only survived, but I admit they were the easiest parties I had ever given. And there were no crafts, so I didn't pull out my glue gun once.

My favorite line from the three days occurred when my daughter was blowing out her candles. "Catherine, you are so lucky to be turning 10. I want to be 10 so bad," her friend Madison said. "But I'm not old enough."

'Tis the Season to Celebrate

Birthday mania taxes creative talent

Because I was born before the annual, bigger-is-better birthday party phenomenon that has gripped my known universe, I had exactly two of them when I was growing up.

There was my 6-year-old party, when my parents rented a projector and tapes from the Buckhead library and a bunch of us little girls in party dresses sat cross-legged on the floor in our playroom, thrilled over the idea that you could watch movies at home.

Then there was my 10-year-old party at Playland, the roller skating rink on Buford Highway, the total hot spot for the elementary school crowd. I had a party with three other kids in my school and we invited the whole class. Despite the hours I spent picking out my prettiest dress and pasting down the cowlick on my bangs with Dippity-Do, the boy I liked skated with another girl, who I once saw squirt lime Jell-O out of her nose but had naturally straight hair.

Somehow our generation of parents has been hoodwinked into this gotta-have-a-birthday-party-each-and-every-year mentality and it has been taxing my creative juices for several years now.

Because my kids were born 11 days apart late summer is birthday season is every year. Our calendar goes like this: Valentine's Day, Easter, Summer, Birthday season, Halloween, Christmas.

Although discussions of the type of birthday parties begins approximately 17 minutes after the one from the previous year ends, we don't seriously get down to business until sometime in the summer. Then the negotiations begin.

One year my daughter decided she wanted a spend-the-night party at the Ritz-Carlton, with transportation via limo and room service for dinner and breakfast. "It would be so easy, mommy," she said. "All you'd have to do is make a few phone calls." That, and write a check for twice my annual salary. What could be simpler?

Another year she casually mentioned how much fun it would be to have her entire class from last year, 72 people, rent out an auditorium somewhere and have a party with a DJ. A real one, not just her daddy with his sound equipment. Or if we couldn't get a DJ, we could just hire a dance instructor who could all come and teach everybody some cool dances. While I agree such an event would be a good time, it's about as likely to happen as me having my next birthday party in Florence, Italy, driven there by limo.

My son is easier to please in this area, as long as the party involves lots of other equally manic 8-year-old boys who come bearing action figure paraphernalia as gifts. But he still believes in cramming a lifetime of parties into one event. One year he was vying for a bowling/going to see "Tarzan"/pool/spend-the-night/pizza party, with chocolate cereal for breakfast. To which I said yes to either No. 1 or No. 2, yes, yes, yes and yuck! but maybe depending on what kind mood I'm in when we go shopping for the party.

But my daughter and I continue to explore options, with most of my suggestions vetoed as too lame, been done before or what's so fun about that! I personally liked my suggestion of the "Hazel" party. Based on the popular TV show, the girls could all come to the party with brooms and dust pans, put on cute little white aprons and hats, and engage in sweeping and dusting competitions. Afterwards they could enjoy the homemade cupcakes they whipped up between the vacuuming and toilet scrubbing.

Surprisingly, she didn't share my enthusiasm for that one.

So we drew up a list of the criteria we both, in some cases grudgingly, agreed on:

1) Must be something not one of her friends has ever done before

2) Must cost less than a mortgage payment

3) Must involve massive intake of sugary and salty processed foods

4) Must be suitably cool for a very-soon-to-be 6th grader

5) Would not involve travel beyond the city limits

6) Would not involve building an addition to the house

After this lengthy and painstaking process was complete, it seemed there were no ideas that met the criteria. While all her suggestions seemed to violate No. 2 big time, all of mine were deemed way too lame for No. 4, especially the weenie roast in backyard. It seemed we were at an impasse until one day we were having lunch at the Varsity and an idea came to me. "We could come here for dinner and then go see a movie at the Fox Theatre," I said.

"That would be a great birthday party," she said.

I breathed a huge sigh of relief.

Now we just have to find a suitable movie. Negotiations will begin anew as we try to find the middle ground between "Shakespeare in Love" and "Wizard of Oz."

I was fairly pleased with our selection of parties another year. My son had a rock climbing party at Atlanta Rocks. It's rather expensive but when you consider that there are no craft projects, house clean up or a sleepless night involved, it makes it easier to write that check.

For my daughter's 14th birthday, we transformed our home into a spa, complete with stations for make-up, cleansing masks, paraffin treatments and hair dos. We served spa food, consisting of appetizer fare, foods that could be eaten daintily with our fingers, without smearing our manicures.

After 14 years of party planning for others, I've decided I need to devote my energies to planning my next birthday party in the spring. Plans are still being considered, but I can tell you now there will be no roller skating, green Jell-O, man-stealing straight-haired girls, sock puppets of any nationality or library videos. I'm thinking more along the lines of what my daughter proposes each year for her party: a limo ride to the Ritz-Carlton, followed by room service. Throw in a few spa treatments and the appropriate companions and you've got yourself a party.

Sending Another Kodachrome Card for Christmas

I don't know about the rest of the country, but here in Georgia (motto: 50th in education, but our peaches are might juicy!) it is customary at Christmas to take an adorable photo of your children, insert said adorable photo into cards and mail it to everyone you've ever had the opportunity to exchange hellos with, including your high school biology lab mate and the clerk at the video rental store.

This charming custom has caused even more stress in my household than trying to set up the nativity scene.One day, we discovered that Joseph had been beheaded, (we think one of the Wise Men was responsible), and efforts to glue, balance or otherwise attach his head were all in vain, resulting in our own private version of "The Nightmare Before Christmas." I finally replaced it with a G.I. Joe head and told the kids a Christmas miracle had occurred.

I consider the Christmas Card Photo Session one of the most painful parts of child raising. Granted, the actual childbirth was more painful, but I only had to do it once for each child and lots of people brought me food. During the many years I've been a mom, we've gone through 187 rolls of film, 27 Christmas outfits, several series of reprints, and lots of protesting and crying on the part of everyone involved.

The first year we took a photo, our daughter was four months old. We propped her up in a rocking chair. We got wonderful shots of her in various phases of toppling over, her large, baby head forcing her from a horizontal to vertical position each time, and a few excellent close-up shots of her diapers.

The year my son was born, we posed him with his three-year-old sister on a small wicker couch in front of the Christmas tree. He had mastered the holding-up-your-head part of being human, but the sitting-up part was still a tricky concept. I helped by reaching over to prop him up while my husband took the picture. The result was that he is tilted forward with his tongue out and his eyes bulging out of his head. With his cute green outfit, he looks not unlike a chubby toad being gigged from behind.

The next year I tried to be artistic. We used an unfurnished room where we draped white sheets for a studio kind of effect. It took five weeks to smock and sew matching Christmas outfits, an hour to set up the room, 45 minutes to get the children dressed in their matching outfits, and 15 seconds for Christopher to throw up on his matching outfit. His was the first case of a flu that afflicted us all in turn. The cards were late that year.

Another year I went for the outdoor shot. We walked to a little park down the street from our house. I sat the children together on a large rock, in a darling brother-sister embrace, Catherine in back with her arms around her little brother. Christopher started bucking back and forth, and I watched in horror as they both fell over backwards off the rock. They lay stunned in a festive red and green heap for a few seconds, then leapt up with howls of outrage.

Now that they are older, gravity is not such a problem. But capturing that award-winning smile is still a challenge. I've tried the usual silly tricks with stuffed animals, performing one-handed skits with Mr. Nini, the stuffed banana, and his sidekick Roo Roo, the one-legged reindeer. Having them say something funny as I snap the picture seems to work best. One year "watermelon spit" and "monkey brains" seemed to work particularly well. Last year I took the winning photo on our deck. I am ashamed to admit that at the time, my children were screaming "butthead" in a volume loud enough to be heard in seven states.

Okay, so it's not language I generally permit, but I had reached the desperation level that every parent knows well. When standards drop. It's the same level of desperation that takes you from the vision of your little darlings beautifully dressed in neatly pressed hand-smocked Christmas outfits with perfectly groomed hair and angelic smiles, to "Well, her tongue isn't sticking out this time and there isn't anything green running down his nose. Let's go with it!"

Another year, I got the kids all dressed up in holiday attire, including handmade Santa hats, and took them to the Festival of Trees, priding myself that we would have a colorful background for our photos. We shot loads of photos in front of the best-decorated trees. Imagine my surprise when I rushed the film in because we were running late that year and discovered I had used black and white film. In addition to the fact that my festive background was now a joke, I found out that the reprints take three times longer and cost three times more. Fortunately I had snapped a shot of them in the parking lot, against the Atlanta skyline, so that year we pretended we were artsy and meant to do that.

Another year my son finally agreed to take off his ever-present Batman hood and dutifully pose for about three minutes, at which point he threw down the stuffed white bear he had in a stranglehold, ran upstairs and hid under his bed. I followed him a little later to see if I could fit two kids under there and if the light was any good.

Each year as I got out my purple glue stick and scissors to paste the photo of my kids onto the cards, I wondered if other parents had been through the same ordeal.

We've long since given up on holiday outfits and festive backgrounds. Next year as long as no one is throwing up, noticeably bleeding or on fire, it's a winner. And if you notice a dancing banana in the foreground, well, I meant to do that.

❄ Holiday Tip

After several torturous years of stressing over the perfect Christmas card, I got smart. Now I select one taken during the year, usually on a family vacation, and just get copies of that.

Memories of Christmas Past

Some holiday memories endure forever,
whether you want them to or not

I have a beautiful red book with "Christmas Memories" engraved on it in gold letters. The first few pages are carefully filled out in red ink with copious memories of the holiday season: parties we attended, restaurants we went to, recipes of treats I made, friends we saw and cute things the kids said. On each page is a family photo in front of the Christmas tree.

As you get further along in the book, the photos are still there. The memories, however, are somewhat abbreviated. The last entry says, "Ate. Drank. Were merry."

So I'm sure I've forgotten a lot of things from Christmas past. But there are several memories that I don't have to write down, those that will stay with me forever, which is not necessarily a good thing.

There is the "I could use an Egg McMuffin but McDonald's is closed" memory. I was making Christmas brunch, and the dozens of scrambled eggs just didn't seem to be cooking, so I turned up the heat. Big mistake. I burned the eggs. We had only three left. I decided to add cheese to try to stretch the eggs for 12 people, but we were low on that as well. Then I remember the cheese ball we'd gotten in a holiday basket. Only a few people complained about the pecans getting stuck in their teeth.

Then there's the "I'd leave this party faster, but I can't sprint in high heels" memory. I had participated in a Christmas Around the World event at my children's preschool. Another woman and I dressed up as characters from other countries and visited the children's classrooms. I was Jultomten from Sweden, a little brownie who helps Santa give gifts. The other woman was Befana, a Christmas witch from Italy.

A few weeks later we went to a Christmas party, and I saw the woman across the dining room table and said hello. Then I said, "Are you a good witch or a bad witch?" She gave me a puzzled look, so assuming she hadn't heard me, I said it louder. When she looked at me with a combination of fear and confusion, I realized she wasn't the witch at all. It was the wrong woman.

Then there's the "At least I got to sit down" memory. When my son was 4, we were in a toy store and he saw a remote control fire engine and decided that was what he wanted for Christmas. There was a huge stack of them. But I had no time when I wasn't with him, so I couldn't go back and get it.

When I finally had a minute I raced back to the store. The stack was gone – replaced by a tower of Barbie doll paraphernalia – hardly an acceptable substitute.

Frantic calls to every store in town confirmed the sad truth. They were sold out. I called the stores in New York. No luck. But they gave me a catalog number to try. I called, and was put on hold for 45 minutes. But I wasn't bored because I got to listen to the jolly sound of little voices singing, "Welcome to Our World, Welcome to Our World of Toys," approximately 5,287 times.

It was worth it because they had it in stock! But after adding on the extra shipping charge to guarantee delivery for Christmas, and after buying the 28 size D batteries it required to make the ladder extend to a knocking-picture-off-the-table level and an ear-piercing sound that attracted dogs all over the neighborhood, we could have made a sizable down payment on a real fire engine.

My all-time favorite Christmas memory is from 1986. We had been trying to have a baby for a long time and had been through all the emotional stress that entails, as well as several way-not-fun-and-oh-so-intrusive medical tests. I went to the doctor on Dec. 23 to get the results of yet another test. Just for the heck of it, I asked for a pregnancy test. The doctor came in the office and said those two magic words, "You're pregnant."

I really didn't believe him, and was sure that the nurse had mixed up my urine sample with that of the woman in front of me, who looked to be about nine months pregnant.

When my husband came home from work I asked him to sit on the couch with me. I pointed to the mantle and said, "We are going to need three stockings up there next year." He looked at me with that "am-I-in-the-Twilight-Zone" look on his face. "Why?" he asked. "We'll need one for the baby," I said.

So that year, I didn't drink, but boy did I eat, and boy was I merry.

A Mom's Letter to Santa

A shameless plea to the big-bearded fellow for
some holiday help

Dear Santa,

Remember me? The one who sent you several letters in the late '60s on Snoopy stationery? (The ones where Lucy always had a black mustache, and Charlie Brown had a red Afro, thanks to annoying artistic embellishments of my little brother.)

Despite all those letters, I never did get that trampoline, Santa, but that's not why I'm writing. See, I'm all grown up now and have two children of my own. And it occurred to me that you and I have a lot in common: It seems we both have children making a lot of demands on us, and are expected to perform super-human feats. So, I thought you would really understand my position and help me out. Could you consider adding a grown-up to your route this year? Here's what I want for Christmas:

1. 87 addressed Christmas cards. I've included a photo of my kids from three years ago that really turned out relatively well (which means no bodily fluids are visible, the grape-juice stains around the mouth are mostly hidden and the sullen expression on my son's face could

almost be mistaken for a spiritual trance of some sort). So all you have to do is have one of your graphic-designer elves age them three years and put them in trendy holiday attire. While you're at it, can you fix that random curl on the left side of my son's hair?

The addresses for the recipients are attached. Well, okay, this list is also three years old, so could you have another elf search the net for the correct addresses? The Hughans moved to Connecticut this year and I don't have their current address.

2. Wrapped age-appropriate presents for nine nieces and nephews, ranging in ages from 9 months to 19, mailed to Dallas, Kansas City, San Jose, St. Louis and San Francisco. No socks, underwear or anything remotely educational, please.

3. Six large batches of fudge in holiday tins mailed to all elderly relatives, and 12 small batches of fudge wrapped to give as teacher presents. Please follow my secret family recipe for "Jan's Fabulous Fudge," which is conveniently printed on the back of the marshmallow fluff, only they call it Fantasy Fudge, and make tags for the teacher presents that read, "To my favorite teacher."

4. One honey-baked ham for Christmas brunch and three dozen eggs. On second thought, better make it six dozen in case I burn the scrambled eggs the first time around, which I did seven years ago and am doomed to be reminded of for the rest of my life. (Note to everybody in my family: It was a mistake! And I thought I was pretty creative with my use of cheese, peppers, granola and leftover banana-bread crumbs so that the three remaining eggs could feed 12 people.)

5. Four really beautiful, flattering outfits that a) match the mysterious, yet commonly used phrase "festive attire," for Christmas parties; b) are revealing enough to be flattering, but cover enough to keep me warm; and c) don't require high heels. (Also, no embroidered elves or teddy bears, please.)

6. One gift under $20 for my Book Club for our heated gift exchange. Every year we all bring gifts, and then we each draw a number and celebrate the true spirit of Christmas by taking turns opening a gift, stealing gifts from each other, and openly criticizing the gifts our friends brought. Oh, and we also laugh hysterically at gift exchanges from previous years and remembering who got stuck with what. Possibly the low point was the mockery we made of Susie's present last year, which was a lovely blue plate with, ironically, a saying about friendship painted on it.

So, Santa, if you could just help me out with these few things, I'll handle the rest - the tree buying and decorating, the gingerbread-house building, the family gift-buying, the present-wrapping, the making spirits bright and even the wassailing.

And hey, there's an extra quart of eggnog in it for you, just the way you like it, and I'll even forget about the whole trampoline thing.

Season's Shenanigans

Creatures stirred, dogs ate trees
and refused makeovers

For you this might have been the holiday season that Aunt Rita finally quit sending you footie pajamas, now that you're 31, or the year your mother learned to take a photograph that included people's heads rather than close-ups of their kneecaps.

For my family, this past Christmas will forever be known as the year Our Dog Ate the Christmas Tree.

We got our tree early this year. My daughter insists we go to Hastings on Peachtree St. so we get "the entire Christmas experience" which consists of them walking around in the frigidly cold lot looking at rows of trees while I stay huddled inside eating the free delicious popcorn, drinking warm apple cider and trying to teach the parrots to say "partridge in a pear tree," venturing out only long enough to agree hurriedly with their selection of a tree.

Soon after the tree was back home and safely in its stand, I walked into the family room and saw several piles of mutilated bark shavings on the floor. I immediately fingered Riley as the culprit. I think he was expressing his frustration. A lot of Christmas goodies had been coming our way and yet he was stuck with dry dog food, morning and night. I figure he decided enough was enough – he was taking a bite out of the next thing to come in the door. I swept up the shavings and put him safely in his crate.

The next morning when I came downstairs I was greeted with a fat-faced dog. My puppy's face had swollen up to the size of a beach ball. Although we were all concerned, we did have to laugh a little at his chipmunk-like appearance, but he did not seem at all amused.

After consulting the vet, I gave him Benadryl. She mentioned that I needed to make sure he didn't have trouble breathing. So I cancelled all my plans for the day to stay home and listen to my dog breathe, which ranks somewhere between flipping your mattress and recaulking your bathtub on the excitement scale.

I talked to the vet's office several more times that day and finally decided not to take him in to see her. But late in the afternoon, I came downstairs and found him with one eye totally swollen shut and the other as red as a Santa suit. He looked like Rocky after a particularly brutal boxing match, and I half expected him to raise his paws and yell out "Adrian!"

We raced him down to the vet, and she thought it might be an allergic reaction, possibly to his eating the Christmas tree. After he had a steroid shot and rousing playtime with their three-legged cat named Squash, we headed back home where he recovered nicely.

It's a good thing because we needed his services on Christmas Eve. Just as we were all settling down for a long winter's nap, (with me opting *not* to wear a kerchief) my daughter yelled up the stairs, "Mom!" in that there's-something-really-bad-going-on tone of voice. I ran downstairs to be confronted with a scurrying mouse, who was blatantly disregarding the story where it *clearly states* that his role is to not be stirring. He was stirring all over our kitchen and hallway. But Riley was on the case, and before we even had a chance to suggest to the mouse that he take his stirrings elsewhere, he pounced on the little critter, knocking over a stool and coming dangerously close to decimating our lovingly decorated gingerbread house.

Later I heard of another pet-related holiday mishap. Some teenage girls wanted to take a picture of themselves in front of the Christmas tree, and wanted their dog to be Rudolf, which of course meant smearing Righteous Red lipstick on his nose. But the dog, resistant to the makeover, kept licking the lipstick off, and they kept reapplying. The fun continued until the dog threw up the Righteous Red lipstick all over the Christmas presents. I didn't hear if they caught that lovely piece of Christmas magic on film.

Our own attempt to photograph our fat-faced dog didn't really turn out, so the episode of The Dog Eating the Christmas Tree will just have to live on in memory. We made an agreement with Riley for next year: he doesn't eat the Christmas tree and we don't make him wear lipstick.

New Year's Resolutions –

*Fewer resolutions, longer timeframe increase
possibility of achieving goals*

There is a very simple formula to follow if you want to actually keep your New Year's resolutions: decrease the number of resolutions and increase the time frame. Who says you have to do everything in a year? Three resolutions in five years works much better. I'm the mother of one teenager (14) and one "pre-teen" (11), as he insists on being referred to, so my resolutions relate to surviving the coming years. Although all is going fairly smoothly right now, I figure it's just a matter of time before I kiss the remains of my sanity goodbye, with sincere hopes of recovering it sometime within the next three presidential administrations.

1) I want to survive both children getting drivers' licenses. Is it just me or does it seem at each stage of parenting you can't even imagine the next one? It started before my first child was born. When I was pregnant, I found it highly improbable that, despite the history of mankind since the beginning to the contrary, a child would actually come out of me.

Once when my son was a sweet little baby, I was

holding him in my arms on the front porch. A group of three boys, around 9 years old, were walking down the street, engaging in a spitting contest. I looked at my darling little bundle and didn't believe he would ever be old enough to walk, much less spit that far. At the age of 11, he can quite readily spit and perform other bodily activities, often with sound effects, much to his own amusement.

So I'm well aware that my children actually do progress to the next phase. But yet, I still can't imagine the next one. Right now I'm in the can't-imagine-they-will-ever-drive-a-car phase.

In five years I will have two children who could actually have licenses to drive a car. I'm working on creative solutions for this one, though. Being in the newspaper business, I thought about bribing our production department to do a mock-up front page with an article announcing that the driving age has been raised to 27. Or I could tell them that the DMV is only open for three hours every other Tuesday during months that have a T in them. But they're pretty smart kids and wouldn't fall for it. Besides, their friends would probably rat me out.

2) Convince my daughter that it is possible to survive sharing a bathroom with her brother. Here is the conversation we have about once a month, usually after she visits one of her many friends who has her own bathroom.

"My friend has her own bathroom!" she says, as soon as she gets in the car.

"That's nice. She's lucky, isn't she?" I say.

"When can I have my own bathroom? I hate sharing a bathroom with my brother! Do you know what he does?" (Insert latest bathroom offense here.)

"You know, I shared a bathroom with two brothers growing up," I say.

"And did you like that? Do you want me to go through that?" she says.

So I'll continue my efforts to convince her that not only will she survive the hardship of sharing a bathroom, but it will actually prepare her for college, and eventually for marriage. My guess is, though, that her marriage vows will include, "I promise to love and honor you and all that other stuff, as long as we never share a sink."

3) Speaking of bathrooms, I again add my annual resolution relating to same: I will take an uninterrupted bath.

This may not sound like an unattainable goal, or even worthy to be included in the resolution category, but if you have children, you know what I'm talking about. In my house the bathtub is second only to the telephone as a kid magnet.

One evening I tried to escape to what I thought would be the private confines of my bathtub. Soon after I sunk in, my first visitor arrived. My son came in, pushing his fire engine, accompanying it with the screeching "wee-oh, wee-oh" sounds that only persons with a Y chromosome are able to make. He wheeled it up to the tub, demonstrated the remote control ladder, and showed me how Fireman Dave could put out a fire in the tub. I thanked him and told him I'd be sure to give him a holler if my herbal conditioner spontaneously combusted.

When he left, I got out and jiggled the lock, a temperamental one that requires the manual dexterity of a

Venetian lace maker. Seconds later I heard the house-rattling knock of a child, the force of which caused tidal waves in the bathtub.

"Mommy!" my daughter yelled through the door. "Look at the picture I made!"

"I'll look later. I'm taking a bath."

Silence. A few seconds later I saw a slip of paper emerging from under the door.

"See?" she yelled.

"I can't see if from here," I said. "I'll look at it later."

A minute later, I looked up to see a long wooden dowel thrust under the door, pushing the prized picture into my view.

I admired her artwork, as well as her ingenuity, and resolved to invest in a deadbolt.

4) I will survive the anticipated diminished communication of having a teenage son. Although they may spend five hours on the phone with their friends, teenage boys tend to communicate with grown-ups through a series of grunts and shrugs, and although I'm sure I could learn to interpret them, I'm hoping we can still carry on conversations made up of real words, and maybe even occasionally a real sentence. But he'll probably want to talk just when I don't want to listen – like when I'm finally trying to take that bath.

Here Comes Those
Tears Again

This month is Mother's Day, but you won't find me getting all sentimental about it. Not that I don't enjoy the homemade cards and the once-a-year breakfast in bed. Or the presents that are carefully selected that afternoon at the drugstore down the street. Who wouldn't get a thrill from receiving another folding umbrella, some strawberry lip-gloss and a leftover Easter Pez dispenser?

It's just that the more moving moments of motherhood for me come at more unpredictable times. And I definitely cry more now that I'm a mother.

At first I blamed it on extreme fatigue. Once when my daughter was about three months old I was standing in the kitchen making roast beef sandwiches and began to sob uncontrollably. My husband, somewhat puzzled about the sorrow that could be found in a little deli meat and mustard, inquired what was wrong.

"Nothing, I'm very happy," I sobbed, while wiping my face with one of those transparent sheets they pack lunch meat in.

The truth was that I'd had about 37 minutes of sleep

in the past three months and was barely standing. But even after resuming somewhat normal sleep patterns, the crying thing continued.

I had quit my full-time job at the High Museum of Art when my daughter was born, but continued to work two afternoons a week while my mother took care of her. The first time I dropped her off and drove away I was barely to the corner when I looked over and the sight of her empty car seat set me off. I cried all the way to Midtown, then tried to fix my makeup with a dried-up baby wipe I found under the seat.

Then there was the first time she bled. We were strolling around downtown when I lifted the stroller off the curb and she fell out onto the street. I swooped her up and then noticed a small cut on her arm. She was totally calm, but there I stood on Peachtree Street, holding her in my arms, tearing up at hurting my child, and wondering if I should take off my blouse or my underwear to make a tourniquet to stem the three drops of blood that were oozing out.

I had another child and the next few years flew by in a messy, swirling chaos. I believe I toughened up a little as I learned children survive cuts and even thrill to the chance to put on a Casper the Ghost neon Band-Aid, and love the opportunity to pull Boo-Boo Bunny, the washcloth-covered plastic ice cube, out of the freezer.

(Although they've outgrown him, I still have him and pulled him out recently when I ran into the dryer door and whacked my shin. Somehow his smiling terry cloth face did make me feel better.) I also came to view empty car seats as a symbol of freedom, not a cause for sadness.

Before I knew it, it was the summer before my daughter started kindergarten. Every time I thought of her going to "the big white school" as she called it, I got misty-eyed. The first day of school I led her to her classroom, went and sat in my car and cried. This time I had to use an old sock puppet I found in the back seat to dry my eyes.

I know I'm not alone in this. A friend of mine was taking her daughter around to visit different schools. While waiting at one school she picked up their high school annual, and begin to tear up while looking at the pictures of the seniors and reading their quotes and thinking of them going off to college. "These weren't even my children," she said embarrassed. "I don't even know these children!"

Soon I'm in for a real test. My daughter graduates from elementary school. Maybe they can stick all us sentimental moms together for support, setting up crying or non-crying sections.

But to make matters worse, the very next day she leaves for her first trip away from home. For two weeks. She's almost 12 years old and we've never been apart that long. For her sake, I'm bracing myself to be strong and dry-eyed when we say good-bye at the airport.

But this time I'm be going prepared. This time I'm taking a box of tissues. And just for good measure, Boo-Boo Bunny is coming to the airport with me. His ears are perfect for fixing eye makeup.

Theme Park Terror

How to lose your dignity, your shoes,
and your lunch for just $50 a day

It's unclear to me why people insist on seeking the sheer terror of theme park rides when all you have to do is get on a major Atlanta highway day or night for the same death-defying experience. But no, we insist on traveling hundreds of miles to pay $50 or more for a ticket, stand in line, and then be scared witless while enjoying the sensation of having a stranger scream in your ear and grab your thigh with sweat-covered claws, an experience I thought I left behind with fraternity dances in college.

I recently had my own personal thrill, as my daughter goaded me into riding the Incredible Hulk Coaster at Universal's Islands of Adventure in Orlando.

Our first ride there was The Amazing Adventures of Spider-Man, possibly one of the best rides ever in the history of the world. After winding your way through a newspaper office, The Daily Planet, which I can tell you from first-hand experience can be a very scary place indeed, you put on 3-D glasses and hop on board the ride, which swings you through the city, thwarting attacks left, right, front and back. There's even fire involved.

That wasn't enough for my thrill-seeking daughter, who had her eye on the scariest roller coasters I've ever seen. But I had sworn off roller coasters after an encounter I had with the Rock-N-Rollercoaster Starring Aerosmith at Disney's MGM Studios a few years ago.

I had waited in line, which took us through a visit to G-Force Records, then boarded the 24-passenger "limo" that raced Aerosmith and us to the concert. When I say race, we went from *0-60 mph in 2.8 seconds*, with a force of five Gs, which is two more than astronauts experience on a shuttle launch, and then went through three inversions with rock concert lighting and an Aerosmith soundtrack blasting through 120 speakers. I still count that as the worst few minutes of my life, and I've sat through the beginning of a Creed concert and been to Chuck E. Cheese on a Friday night.

But at my daughter's urging we headed up the entrance to the Dueling Dragons, a pair of coasters that soar up to 125 feet. I made it halfway up the walkway until, coming closer to the screaming passengers and roar of the coasters, I chickened out. The worst was taking the Walk of Shame back down the ramp. I thought about holding up my cell phone and claiming to the people I passed that I was a doctor and had just gotten paged, faking an appropriate look of regret. When I asked a worker where the exit was, he said, "I wish we had one, but no one has ever come back out." Just a little theme park humor.

Towards the end of the day we made our way through Seuss Landing, where the scariest thing was the prices on the merchandise for sale in the multiple gift shops. We enjoyed a relaxing ride on the Caro-Seuss-El, a merry-go-round with Seuss-like creatures. I thought I was home free.

But my daughter had one last ride in mind. The Incredible Hulk Roller Coaster. Somehow I found myself agreeing to go on a ride that looks like those twirly circles you make when you take a pen and try to get it to write.

It is *so* not a good sign when you have to get a locker to store your stuff in just to go on a ride. I tried to hide my fear in there as well, but it refused to leave my body.

It didn't make me feel any better that a little boy, about 8 years old, was jumping up and down in excitement to get on the ride. His mother confessed to a slight nervousness, and said she would probably scream the whole time.

"I'll be right there with you," I said. "I'll be yelling too."

I was wrong. I did not scream, primarily because screaming involved breathing, a function I was unable to engage in, being literally frozen with fear. Eyes squeezed shut, hands clamped to the restraints in a death grip; I sat immobile as the ride took us from 0-40 in two seconds and through seven inversions.

I remained speechless as we wobbled down to our locker to retrieve our belongings. But my sense of balance and any tiny remainder of thrill seeking in my personality I left behind at Universal Islands of Adventure. From now on, any thrills I need I'll get from some competitive bidding on E-Bay.

Five

The Teen Years

Battening Down the Hatches for the Teenage Years

It's official. This month I become the parent of a teenager. I suppose it was inevitable this day would come, but I'm a firm believer in the power and beauty of denial and preferred to think of these coming years as . . . well, I just preferred not to think about them. Besides, between making Batman capes for birthday parties and keeping the household stocked with an endless supply of Honey Nut Cheerios and #2 pencils, there has been little time for contemplation of the future.

But the future is here. We have been teasing about it. "Well, maybe you won't be one of those teenagers," I said to my daughter. "Mom, every parent wants to think that their child won't be one of those teenagers," she said.

It's been pretty smooth sailing so far with her. She is one of the sweetest children I know. Once last year, in one of my moments of losing it over the abysmal state of our house, I stormed upstairs and ranted about how I would have to work for hours just to find the floor. A few minutes later she tentatively came up the stairs. She was holding a Diet Coke in one hand, and a plate of pimiento cheese and crackers in the other. "Here, mom, I thought you'd need some energy for your work," she said. "I'll clean downstairs." She continues to charm and delight me on a daily basis, and is a great companion.

But we got an inkling of what lay ahead the summer after fifth grade. She went to France for a two-week trip with her school. I picked her up from the airport one Friday afternoon, and shortly after our tearful reunion, she went to sleep.

The next morning I went to work out and called home to check on her. "She is in her room sulking," my husband said. "She said there is nothing to do in Atlanta." The child had been home, conscious, for approximately 37 minutes, and was already bored. There were a few more episodes that summer when life was horrible because our family room couch was embarrassingly ugly, she has to share a bathroom with her brother as well as every guest that walks in the house, and why didn't we have a big basement with a big-screen TV?

That period was mercifully short-lived, but intense enough for me to realize I'll have to find some more patience somewhere. The problem is I used it all up in the early '90s when I had two toddlers, and my supply doesn't seem to have replenished itself.

And my knowledge of teenagers is somewhat limited. What I know comes from having been one more than a few years ago, (before cell phones, computers, and shopping malls the size of Rhode Island, so it really doesn't count) and having heard stories at parties from older parents who were dealing with driver's licenses and dating issues, which is usually when I would excuse myself to get some more cheese dip. (Denial is easier when one is fortified with cheese dip.)

Here's what I do know about teenagers:

When motivated, they can be crafty. In "Dear Abby" there was a series of articles about getting teenagers to observe a curfew, while allowing the parents to get some sleep. One parent came up with what I thought was a brilliant idea: set an alarm clock for curfew time. When the teen comes home, he turns it off and the parents get to sleep. If he doesn't come home, the alarm goes off and the parents know he has missed his curfew.

Then some teenagers wrote in. "My parents did that. I would pay my sister a dollar to turn it off," one said. "I would come home, turn it off, then go back out," said another.

Although you drive them places, cook their meals, buy and wash their clothes, they sometimes prefer to believe you don't really exist. And speaking at all in front of their friends is strongly discouraged. I'm not sure if the monosyllabic deep grunt, perfected by a 15-year-old boy in California in 1992 and quickly adopted by teenage boys nationwide, is acceptable in this situation. My guess is that any contact with their friends should be accompanied by a slight nod and a speedy exit.

They are no longer distracted, or bought off, by a cookie or brownie. This one will be particularly hard on me, as I've based a large part of my parenting strategy on the power of freshly baked goodies. However, I am still counting on the allure of the magnificent aroma of the just-out-of-the-oven chocolate chip cookie to at least get her out of her room if she's been in there a few days and

I've forgotten what she looks like.

So I have a lot to learn. But to paraphrase George Clooney in "A Perfect Storm," whatever happens, "It will be a heck of a ride!"

Happy 13th birthday, Catherine. I love you and thank God for you every day. I'm here when you need me. And I'm here even when you think you don't.

✐ Tip for Teens

One of the sadder aspects of your child becoming a teen is giving up those discount meals. I write a restaurant column for a newspaper in Atlanta and always get a kick out of the holiday brunch notices I get. I once calculated that brunch at the Ritz-Carlton for a family of two parents with two teenagers was approximately the cost of a car payment on a luxury car.

Many restaurants will still give your younger teen an item off the kid's menu. Another alternative is the drive-through. As for Easter brunch, buy a honey-baked ham and eat at home!

✐ Tip for Teens

If you're having trouble bonding with your teen, pull out those old high school yearbooks and photos. You'll both be laughing uproariously in no time.

A Walk Up the Street
Takes Us Back in Time

W e live in a city where you can take a week's vacation and return to find your neighborhood Mexican restaurant has been replaced by a Blockbuster, the cute little house down the street has been demolished and a McMansion is taking its place, and the dry cleaners you've gone to for 15 years has been turned into a nail salon. So it's rather refreshing to find a place that never changes. And hasn't changed since the Kennedy administration, when it first opened.

West Barber Shop is such a place.

For years now, my son and I have been strolling up to West Barber Shop on Howell Mill Road to get his hair cut. Our signal to go is when he declares "I can't stand it any more!" while threatening to cut off his own "sideburns" or when even a walnut-sized application of mega gel is insufficient to tame his stick-up-hair down to a non-Alfalfa, socially acceptable state.

He refers to it as the Old Geezer Barber Shop. (No

offense intended. It's just that when you're 11 years old, anyone past the age of a Backstreet Boy can qualify for old geezer status.)

We've got the ritual down. He hops up on one of the four barber chairs and I settle down and try to find something current to read. This is definitely high-testosterone territory, I've never even seen another woman in there, so I try to keep a low profile. I resist the urge to chat with the men folk, saying something like, "Hey, it says in this issue of Newsweek that man landed on the moon. Can you beat that?" and refrain from using the words "cute", "adorable" or "darling" when describing the desired hairstyle to the barber.

The walls are covered with dark paneling, and lined with framed black-and-white photos of Atlanta's past. They used to have a black and white TV, further enhancing its "Pleasantville" atmosphere, but it's been upgraded to color.

Once we were there and I got to listening as an elderly, jug-eared man chatted away to his barber about old days in the neighborhood and his dearly departed wife Virginia. Soon I figured out that it was none other than our very own PickRick-Restaurant-owning, ax-handle-wielding, backward bicycle-riding former governor Lester Maddox. Although he no longer lives in the neighborhood, he was the first occupant of the Georgia governors' mansion on West Paces Ferry, just a piece down the road, when he was governor from 1967-71 and his infamous PickRick Restaurant was just up the way on Hemphill near Georgia Tech.

Bob usually cuts my son's hair, and we have the

same conversation each time we go. He asks my son his name, and he says "Christopher." Then Bob says, "I've got a grandson named Christopher."

After he finishes snipping away, up over the ears, but not too short, he looks at me. "How does this look, Mama?" he asks, the only person on the planet to address me that way. Then Christopher hops down, and Bob offers him some jellybeans from a small glass container near the old cash register.

On our last visit, I asked Bob how long he had been there and how old the shop is. "Well, the chairs say 1960, so I figure that's about when it opened," he said. "I've been here 18 years." According to Bob, Mr. West was the second owner of the shop, but sold it and moved to Tennessee, where he is still cutting hair.

A few weeks ago, when my daughter and I were getting our hair cut at New Talents in Buckhead, an affordable division of the trendy Van Michael Salon, I briefly entertained the thought of taking my son there as well. My idea was met with vehement, horrified disapproval. "You *cannot* bring him here," Catherine said.

Apparently there are some still some gender-related absolutes in life: Girls go to salons, boys go to barber shops.

I can live with that, I supposed. But the guys have it better. I've never gotten jellybeans at a salon.

Fried and Convicted: The Tale of a Joke That Backfired

School starts back this week, and parents everywhere can enjoy getting back into the routine, meeting the new teachers and hoping that the other kids at school will forget about that practical joke last spring that backfired.

Well, that last part may just apply to me.

My kids go to the same school in this area that I went to. And although it's been a few decades since I was there, I still have wonderful memories of their delicious fried chicken, served with soft white rice and salty green beans on a plastic school tray, just the way Mother Nature intended it.

Whenever my daughter tells me they had fried chicken for lunch, I jokingly say, "Would it have killed you to just have slipped one little old breast in your pocket and brought it home to me?" Her response was always the same – a slightly exasperated sigh, and a look that just stops short of incredulous eye rolling.

Last spring I attended a Celebration of Learning

event for the eighth grade, followed by a luncheon. What a thrill I had when I entered the same old cafeteria from my high school days and saw tray after tray of beautiful brown fried chicken!

After indulging myself in its delectable greasiness, along with the rice and green beans of course, we headed out of the cafeteria. My daughter ran on up ahead, but one of her friends was right beside me as we passed by the food tables, which still held piles of perfect poultry.

"Hey," I said. "Let's play a trick on Catherine. Tell her that I grabbed some chicken on the way out and stuffed it in my purse."

It seems I seriously underestimated the acting ability of my daughter's friend, and her talent for telling a story without breaking into giggles, a rare ability for a 14-year-old girl.

That afternoon when Catherine came home, she confronted me with the story. "Mom, tell me it's not true. Kids at school said you took chicken from the cafeteria."

"You believed that?" I said, laughing. "That was just a joke on you." Holding up my tiny fake Kate Spade purse, I pointed to it. "There isn't even enough room for a tiny wing in here!"

"Well, she sounded like she was telling the truth. And then people in my next class started talking about it. Soon everyone was asking me if the story was true."

My laughter disappeared, quickly replaced by horror. My poultry pilfering in the purse prank had backfired! Now the entire junior high at my daughter's school thinks I'm a chicken thief. From there the story would probably spread faster than kudzu in a field of junkyard cars, and by tomorrow all the parents would know as well.

What possible solution could there be? I briefly entertaining the notion of moving far away before the start of the next school year, but that seemed a tad extreme, and besides, what if they forgot to forward my mail and I missed the invitation for the annual alumni Fried Chicken dinner in the fall?

A mass e-mail to all parents in the 8th grade was another possibility, but held its own logistical complications. What would the subject line be? "Alleged poultry pilferer protests" or "I am not a breast burglar!" And the risk of being branded a genuine lunatic, in addition to a chicken thief seemed rather high. It was best to do nothing.

So here's hoping that the start of a new school year brings me a clean record.

And I'm sure that when I attended that meeting at school the other night, it was just my imagination that when the other mothers saw me, they quickly formed a line and linked elbows in front of the food table. That's okay – I paid a 7th grader \$1 to go get me some chocolate chip cookies.

✎ Tip for Teens

Teens don't always respond well to lots of questions about what is going on in their lives. Allow time in the day for conversation and let them introduce topics. Ideally, this is during family dinnertime. My son and I also take my dog for a walk almost every day, and that's when I hear what is going on in his life. Establish your own daily ritual and you'll be amazed at what you'll learn and how you will stay connected.

First Dances
and Discarded Dresses

My daughter recently attended her first dance. As parents are so prone to doing, I told her about my first dance, despite the almost universal belief of teenagers that nothing in their parents' experiences could possibly be relevant to their own lives.

I was in 8th grade and vividly remember the yellow-print one-piece shorts outfit I had sewn myself, marvelously coordinated with the macramé belt I had also made. This was about midway through my intense macramé period, and I spent hours passionately weaving strings to create plant holders, belts and purses. In one particularly ambitious spurt, I even attempted a doublewide hammock, where I would cozy up with all those cute boyfriends I would undoubtedly be collecting now that I was in high school.

Anyway, I eagerly attended the 8th-grade dance, a good place to begin collecting boyfriends, or so I thought.

I did make an intimate connection – with a hard chair on the gym floor. No one asked me to dance. Not one boy even got close enough to admire the fine hand-work of my macramé belt. After the final strains of "Smoke on the Water" signaled the end of the dance, I left, resolving not to attend another one until I had a date. It was the low point of what, in retrospect, was the low point of my life – the entire 8th grade year.

In 9th grade I found my first boyfriend, a 10th-grad-er at another school. (It is assuredly of no coincidence that by then I had moved past my macramé period, stopped wearing yellow shorts outfits, got my braces off and got contacts.) Scott asked me to the fall dance, and I was thrilled.

My mom and I shopped all the stores at the then-new Perimeter Mall. We found a long, black dress with a plaid bodice, puffy sleeves and a plaid ruffle at the bottom. I don't remember much about the dance, and the boyfriend didn't last much longer. He stopped calling and I heard that he had developed some chemistry with his lab partner. The dress I still have.

Recently my daughter and I pulled my old dresses out of the attic, looking for possibilities for a Halloween costume for her. She loved the green gingham dress my mom had made me for a debutante party on the riverboat at Stone Mountain Park, so I excitedly looked for my other ones.

I triumphantly pulled out that old black dress from 9th grade first. "Here it is," I said, "the one I wore to my first dance!" I said excitedly as I held it up and twirled around.

She looked at it with the same expression she had when I had tried to feed her strained peas as a baby. "So that's the dress you wore when no one asked you to dance?" she asked, her eyebrows raised, in a that-would-certainly-make-sense kind of way.

"No, a boy had actually asked me," I said haughtily. Upon looking at the dress again, I'll admit that it was a touch Morticia-esque. I hastily retreated back into the recesses of the attic to find the prom dresses, sure she would appreciate the memories wrapped up in them.

"Here's one of my prom dresses," I said, pulling out the yards of bright green dotted Swiss, the halter dress with a ruffle around the bottom and a matching shawl I had worn my senior year.

"You wore *that*?" she said, even more horrified than she had been at the first one. Although I could see that a positive response might cause her to question many things about her mother and perhaps face up to unpleasant truths about my past, I could not shield her.

"Yes, I did," I said. "And I had a cute date for the prom, too!" I thought it best to leave out the detail that he had worn a green tux, for fear of forever losing any credibility in matters of style.

"Why did you save these things?" she asked. I was wondering the same thing. I supposed I was saving them for my daughter. But I pictured her looking at them admiringly, and asking questions about life as a teenager "back then" rather than trying to reconcile these fashion atrocities with the mother she knew.

I suppose I should haul all those old dresses to the Nearly New, where they could provide an even greater segment of the population with a good laugh. But I decided to pack them back up as a reminder. A reminder that although boys may come and go, the memories of our first dance will live forever, and that we can't always shield our children from our past. Even a past that includes macramé belts, dotted Swiss prom dresses, and puffy-sleeved gowns.

✐ Tip for Teens

If you're having trouble getting your child to remember chores, try deducting money from his or her allowance for each chore not done. I also hereby grant you permission to deduct allowance if the chore gets done, but is accompanied by heaping amounts of attitude.

✐ Tip for Teens

Don't take it personally when your child wants to spend more time with his friends and less with you. That's a good thing! He is learning important social skills, and let's face it, do you really want him still living with you when he's 27?

✐ Tip for Teens

We've found that a monthly allowance works better than weekly. They are old enough to start budgeting their money, and I only have to remember to go to the bank once a month.

☺ Web Wit

You spend the first two years of their life teaching them to walk and talk. Then you spend the next sixteen telling them to sit down and hush.

☺ Web Wit

Mothers of teens now know why some animals eat their young.

Going the Distance

Run with daughter a battle to
maintain self-esteem

lthough I like to think my behavior is generally governed by logic, and I learn from my mistakes, there are occasions when my actions can claim no such rational basis. In such cases, I may even act in self-destructive ways. This is the only explanation for my recent decision to go running with my daughter.

My daughter had been running a mile and a half at school every week during P.E. At the end of the quarter, her teacher recommended she continue doing so, and could get credit if she ran after school.

So one day I suggested we go run together. I said this because:

a) It would be something fun for us to do together, besides going to Abercrombie & Fitch again to see if those ridiculously over-priced pants were on sale yet.

b) I pictured us running leisurely together on the beautiful nature trail at her school, breathing fresh air, getting exercise and enjoying a mother-daughter chat.

c) I had forgotten that I would rather lie on a bed of

Legos, surrounded by black-light Jimmy Hendrix posters, and be forced to listen to an endless track of "Tie a Yellow Ribbon" by Tony Orlando and Dawn than ever go running again.

In high school I gave it a shot - which means I braved the 27 hills in my neighborhood for two agonizing days, listened to the loud protests of my aching knees and promptly gave it up. (The only exception I ever made to my no-running policy was in college, when I was so angry at my then-boyfriend for standing me up to go to an "adult" movie with his fraternity brothers, that I ran around the equally hilly streets of Charlottesville, Va., for the entire evening, fueled by the immeasurable energy of a scorned woman.)

So one Sunday afternoon my daughter and I got suitably attired and drove over to her school. The nature trail, which meanders around the football field and next to a stream, was deserted. But as we warmed up, David, an old classmate of mine and business associate of my husband's, showed up with his kids to play on the field. "Just out for a run," I said breezily, as if it were an everyday occurrence.

After a few stretches, we headed into the woods. Within 3.7 seconds my daughter was yards ahead of me, looking back at me quizzically. "Come on, Mom," she said. "What's the hold-up?"

"Just go on ahead," I panted. "I'll meet you at the end." The hold-up was that with just a few steps, my total hatred of this running thing had returned. Not only that, but I was struggling to continue, and had slowed down to a spirited walk.

Could I really be this out of shape? Hadn't I been

going to work out at least twice a week for years, walking the treadmill and keeping up in step classes with all those girls with the sorority T-shirts?

But I had to lay aside these disturbing thoughts because just then, with great horror, I realized that there were gaps between the trees where David could see me while he played on the field. Reluctant to add the emotion of humiliation to the already overwhelming drop in self-image I was feeling, as I approached each gap in the trees, I would rev up and start running energetically again. I even managed an upturned grimace that I hoped would be mistaken as a smile at a distance.

Remembering my run through Charlottesville, I tried to work up some anger at something to fuel me along. Anything. But life was good, and my husband was even cooking dinner that night.

I pushed on, and finally made it. I suggested we walk around the trail, for at least a few minutes of togetherness, (and for me to catch my breath before we climbed the hill back to our car.) Trying to be kind, she pointed out where I had missed a turn and ran a little farther than I should have. About five feet.

"That's why it took you longer, mom," she said.

In spite of my dismal performance, we have plans to go back. I figure at the very least I get some kind of credit for trying - and it's really good for her self-esteem to so thoroughly outdistance her mother. And besides, you can buy a lot of running shorts for what those pants at Abercrombie & Fitch.

Out of the Equation

Tables turn when it comes to helping with math

When I was growing up, they called it "new math." I'm convinced that phrase was invented by a frustrated parent and foisted on the educational system as a way of letting all parents off the hook when they could no longer help us with our homework. "Oh, I don't know how to do it *that* way," they would say. "That's *new* math," then go back to teasing their hair, growing long sideburns and watching "Laugh-In."

Parents these days have no easy way out. Despite my continued claims that the level of her math problems has exceeded my knowledge, she still asks. (The last time I took a math class, I was wearing hip huggers and complaining about having to take typing class with those geeky 9th grade boys, when I knew I would never have a job where I would have to type. I recently read an article where one of those geeky 9th grade boys sold a software company for several million dollars.)

Last year, she asked me to take the number nine four times, do anything I wanted with them, and come up with the number 100. This problem at first mildly interested me, then obsessed me. Ignoring the hungry, increasing anguished pleas of my children about dinner, I went through a house full of #2 pencils trying to figure it out.

A recent episode has potentially cured her forever of asking my assistance. After an extremely exhausting day, I got home late and laid down on my bed, so exhausted I was contemplating whether there were any long-term adverse effects to sleeping in pantyhose, high heels, and whatever traces of make-up left that I'd hastily applied 14 hours earlier. "Mom," I heard from the adjoining office. "I need your help."

I propped myself up, "Come on in," I called, hastily rearranging my priorities from my need for sleep to helping my children, as I'd done a gazillion times before. (Oops, did that sound just a tad martyr-esque?)

She brought her math book in and said, "I have to figure out what comes next in this pattern. J,F,M,A,M,J,J —, —, —."

I stared at it, waiting for a pattern to jump out at me, but the only thing leaping to my mind was that I was really happy I didn't have to go through 7th grade again.

"Let's see," I said. "Where does "J" fall in the alphabet? Maybe that has something to do with it." I began to sing the alphabet song, "A,B,C,D,E,F,J... okay J is the seventh letter in the alphabet." I made a note on her book.

I looked over to see the look of horror, mixed with fear on her face. "What?" I asked, thinking she was embarrassed yet again by my singing. "No one else heard me."

"Mom, that's *not* how it goes," she said. The she sang the alphabet song. With the G,H,I included.

We laughed so hard my high heels fell off, and she went to finish her math. On her own. (I laid on the bed, trying not to contemplate that not knowing the alphabet may be considered a drawback in my profession.)

Since I'm obviously of no use to her with her math problems, and it seems my kids are both way better than me, I'm going to ask them to help me with my problems.

Like these:

Q. If I have two children and they each bring home a slip of paper every third day during September and October with a request for another item for school, how many trips will I have to make to Target before we get all the school supplies needed? Extra credit: Taking into account that the average amount I spend at Target is $87.13 for each trip, will I have enough money leftover to enroll Aunt Edna in the Doily of the Month Club for Christmas?

Q. If two children each wear one pair of white socks a day, the mom wears a pair only when she gets to go work out or take a walk, approximately every 3.8 days, and considering a remainder of four unmatched socks each time, how long will it take her to fold the socks after they sit on the window seat for two weeks? (Hint: she folds socks at the rate of about 2.7 per minute, unless she is on the phone, when it drops to 2.2 per minute.) How many sock puppets can we make with the leftover socks?

And if they come and ask me for help with these problems, I'll just say, "Oh, that's new millennium math. We didn't have *that*."

The Life of Riley

Finding love again at The Humane Society

Yes, folks, love is for sale right. Look no further than 981 Howell Mill Road. That's where you'll find the Atlanta Humane Society.

This won't be an essay about how dogs make the most amazing companions. Or how much we cried when our beloved dog Pepper slipped off her leash and ran out into the street after a walk in Atlanta Memorial Park and got killed by a car. No, this will be a story about us searching for, and finding love again at the Atlanta Humane Society.

We headed out a few weeks after Pepper died, retracing our steps of a few years before, when we found her. This time we knew the drill – head for the adult section and walk up and down the aisles. I had told the kids that we needed an older dog, one that is housebroken. (Which is kind of an interesting term if you think about it. Pepper did more than her share of breaking the house: blasting through the screens on our porch when she saw a squirrel in the front yard, scratching the top of the buffet in the dining room in a maneuver we can only imagine because it's up so high, and scraping all the paint off the louvered doors between the kitchen and the dining room when we wouldn't let her sit under the table during fancy dinners.)

Up and down the aisles we walked, reading the often misspelled, but obviously written with love, descriptions of the dogs and how they got to be there. Most of them didn't include much information; owner moved, found on the highway, didn't get along with other pets. The sound in there was often overwhelming, as the excited barks of so many abandoned dogs echoed through the high ceiling rooms.

After identifying a few of our favorites we found an AHS staff member to let us take our choices on a test drive. Remember in the movie "The Big Chill" when one of the characters says she can tell in the first 15 seconds whether she is interested in a man or not? Well, it takes a little longer with a dog, but not much.

The first couple of dogs were quite lively, but didn't pay too much attention to the children. Then my daughter spied Max, a black lab mix. He was only four months old and we never really figured out why he was in the adult room. "I wanted to get an older dog," I said. "This one is a puppy and he is not housebroken." "Let's just take him out for a minute," my son said.

Although he was frisky enough to be fun, he alternately laid his head on both my kids' laps. Then he walked right to me, looked me straight in the eyes and laid his head on my lap. "You know who the decision maker is, don't you," I said, much to the amusement of the handler. We played with him a little longer, then after a little paper work, and $67 later, he was a member of our family.

Then came the hard part. Finding a name. My son lobbied hard to keep the name "Max" but my daughter protested equally vehemently on the grounds that it is the most common dog name, "not only in this country but in Australia too!" (If you don't believe the Internet, just go to Piedmont Park on a Sunday weekend afternoon and yell "Max!" and see just how overwhelmed with doggy love you'll be.)

Other rejected names were Chip, Strider and Knightly. My daughter liked the name Riley, and after negotiations worthy of the Jordan-Israel Peace Treaty, that became his name.

Like any new relationship, we've had our challenges. We're still working on the house training, and walking him on a leash is like trying to water ski, but without the water. Chewing on my toes while I eat breakfast, eating the rug in my office and biting the heads off innocent stuffed animals are a few other of the unacceptable behaviors. Obedience school should help with that.

He may need a little training in socially acceptable behavior, but he obviously has the life skills to succeed. After all, he talked his way into the adult room at the humane society, and from there it was just a tail wag and a wide-eyed puppy dog stare to work his way into our hearts and our home.

On the Road, We Hope

It's not like I haven't known fear before. I lost my son at Chuck E. Cheese when he was two years old, only to recover him at the bottom of a germ-infested ball pit.

I was once the only woman on a quail-hunting trip to Albany, Georgia (that's not the scary part, although the sight of so many men in plaid shirts and orange hats was a touch frightening). On the way back, our small private plane hit massive turbulence, the visibility was akin to opening up your eyes with your face jammed against your pillow, and I felt like we were inside a tennis ball during a heated match between the Williams sisters.

And I've even tried on bathing suits in a group dressing room.

But there's nothing quite like the terror of sitting in a passenger seat of a car while a person, to whom you gave birth to what seems not that long ago, is in charge of the motion of two tons of steel.

My daughter is learning how to drive.

I, on the other hand, am learning how to fake being calm and in control while saying things like, "Just slowly go between the car and the concrete wall," and "Just steer to the right of the poodle and to the left of the mailbox."

She's doing fairly well so far, and she is taking Driver's Ed at school. The scary thing about that is the teacher *is the same one* I had in high school. How anyone has the nerves to teach generations of Atlanta children how to drive is a mystery to me. When I took her to the school parking lot a few weeks ago to practice, I resisted the temptation to mow down all the orange cones, then yell out, "Hey Mr. M., remember me? You taught *me* how to drive!"

He must have done a decent job, because I'm a fairly good driver, at least when I'm going forward. Out of all the trees in Atlanta, I've only run into one. And I've gotten just one speeding ticket, when I was 16. I had just broken up with my boyfriend and was counting on an afternoon of crying in my room, leaving only briefly to refuel on raw cookie dough and Twinkies, when my mom made me go pick up my brother after tennis practice. In a hurry to resume my project of drawing devil horns and mutant body parts on his side of our prom pictures, I was driving a little too fast and got pulled over. The only good thing is that when I got home and burst into tears about the ticket, I decided to spill the beans about the breakup, so my parents didn't even get mad at me. (Note to teenagers: try to schedule break-ups or blatantly unfair teacher confrontations on the same day as any ticketed driving violations.)

In the category of How Did We Survive Our Childhood, one year a bunch of us piled in my car, a big old former company car of my dad's that could seat most of the female population of the junior class, and drove to Tifton for the basketball championships. When shifting lanes, I'd call to the back seat, "Hey, is it okay to change lanes?"

My friend Margaret would pause from whatever the current chain of gossip was, and say, "Yeah, it's fine."

After the championship, as we were nearing home, she said, "You know all those times you asked me if you could pull over?"

"Yeah?" I said.

"I never looked."

The driving laws in regards to teenagers driving hordes of friends around have gotten stricter since then, and I'm developing a few of my own rules as we go along. Some of these include: no driving on any major highways until you are 25, and no talking on the cell phone except in an emergency. So far this hasn't been an issue because, as she points out to me on a regular basis, "I'm the only one of my friends who doesn't have a cell phone."

My last rule is: No one is allowed to eat Cheetohs in my car. This has nothing to do with driving – I just don't want orange crumbs all over my rear end.

I suppose that teaching her to drive is a little like childbirth: it's a painful process, with a lot of teeth gritting and silent cussin' involved, but you have to look past the pain to the joy part, which in this case is having someone else to do errands for me. Then I'll get her a cell phone too – so I can call her to remind her to pick up some orange juice *and* her little brother after tennis practice.

✎ Tip for Teens

I have absolutely no advice for you for the first time you get in the passenger seat with your child behind the wheel. There is nothing to prepare you for this moment. You could practice running past mailboxes with an inch between you and those rigid metal poles all the while stifling your screams, but you might as well wait for the real thing.

Mollusk Parts and
the Origins of OPEC

Studying for sixth-grade exams

I figured when I took my last English exam in college, stressing about exam pressure was over. With the exception of the occasional nightmare where I show up half an hour late wearing a hand towel to take a test in a German, which I never studied, that has mostly been true. Until the last few weeks of school this year.

I helped my son study for his sixth grade exams. I never took exams in 6th grade and am fairly sure I was still trying to perfect the art of making a puppet out of a paper bag, which I had gloriously failed in kindergarten by drawing the face on the wrong side. But I suppose the theory is that it's never too early to introduce our children to stress, pressure and the invaluable skill of always being in possession of two #2 sharpened pencils.

We started with World Cultures. The exam was on the Middle East, which meant I got to bone up on my geography skills, which are dismal and the sole reason I always lose at Trivial Pursuit. Well, that *and* those pesky sports questions. When I quizzed my son about the way of life in the Middle East in the old days, he told me that the dad always had the final say, a man could have up to four wives and that he only had to recite a phrase to divorce his wife.

"The women were just sock monkeys for the men," he said authoritatively.

I learned that 95 percent of Egyptians live on just five percent of the land. Then I got mad all over again about OPEC and how much power they have and made a wish that one day we can all just tool around in cute little electric cars and show them a thing or two.

Our next topic was Life Science. I didn't even pretend not to be grossed out by the photos of frog innards, the gizzard of a segmented worm and the anus of a mollusk. The winner of the lose-my-lunch photo goes to the hookworm mouth, however. It was almost enough to make me forget my southern roots and quit walking barefoot outside, a chief pleasure of children that not even a few splinters followed by being poked by your mama with a needle can deter.

I then quizzed him on the meaning and spelling of prokaryotic cell, motochondria, phylogeny and endoplasmic reticulum. I could verify the spelling but because he didn't have the answers written down, I just had to take his word for it that he was giving me the correct response. Besides, it certainly sounded like he knew what he was talking about and if that isn't the best skill you can use to prepare you for the rest of your life, I don't know what is.

Then we got to the classification systems for animals.

I learned that Aristotle actually came up with a primitive classification of the animal kingdom, which scientists later guffawed at, which is what they all love to do when they aren't poking at things in labs. Now there are six classifications. It seems every living thing is divided into categories depending on whether we're prokaryotic or eukaryotic*, one or many-celled, we move or don't move and whether we make or catch our own food.

I noticed that as an example of animals, he put down "me!"

"But you don't make or catch your own food," I said. "And sometimes you've been known to sit on the couch for hours without moving."

That remark quite distressed him, but he had a quick comeback. "I made my own sandwich yesterday," he said. "And even when I'm in a video-game zone, I'm moving my thumbs."

After a short discussion of the fact that he had indeed made his own peanut butter sandwich the day before, and a concession that thumb moving qualified as movement, however slight, I agreed that he could remain in the animal classification.

Exams are now over, the pressure is off, and we'll be busy running around barefoot, not carrying number two pencils around. If we get bored, I'll just impress them with my paper bag puppet-making skills, which I have now perfected.

* If you don't know which one you are, check your person carefully for a nucleus. If you don't locate one, you are a prokaryote.

The Exam-ined Life Leads to All-Nighters for Mom

It's exam time at our house. Life is not fun. I had thought I had done everything I could to help: bought a few items of generally verboten junk food, allowed the kids to spread their books and study guides over every surface of the main floor of our house, cleaned up crusty orange fingerprints left on every surface by said junk food, cooked decent dinners and made sure they ate a good breakfast. I even pulled out the old waffle iron for homemade blueberry waffles, and fired up the bread machine because it has been scientifically proven that the smell of fresh baked bread increases the learning capacity of the teenage mind.

(Okay, so I made that one up. Just don't tell my kids , okay?)

I even listened sympathetically and agreed with my son each of the 27 times he complained that exams are evil, unnecessary and place an unfair burden on his 13-year-old shoulders. I tried to make him feel better by pointing out that it could be worse - he could be undergoing some sort of physical exam in which case things get poked and prodded that are more comfortable left alone, but alas, that did nothing to improve his mood.

Then I told him that Socrates had said, "The unexamined life is not worth living." He said, "Well, Socrates obviously never had to take a 7th-grade history exam on the battles of the Civil War," a statement with which I was unable to disagree.

You would have thought what I was doing during my waking hours would have been about all a mom could do. But no, it seems my sleeping hours have been overcome by those dreaded exam dreams.

A few nights ago I dreamed I had a history class but didn't know what room it was in, only that it had a 2 in the room number. Last night I was holed up in a hotel room, constantly eating bowls of Cheerios with strawberries, and desperately trying to locate my exam schedule. Later that night, I dreamed that my Memorial Day was not going to be spent relaxing poolside, but rather studying for an AP chemistry exam.

Although I've often had these dreams in the many years since I graduated from college, in real life I was only late once to an English exam. I still recall the horror of waking up at 9:15 for a 9:00 exam. I remember going into full-blown panic mode and racing up Jefferson Park Avenue to Cabell Hall, bed-hair flying and tears held in check until I could plead my case. As I recall, my teacher allowed me to finish the exam.

I decided to do a little research on exam dreams, which are quite common. I didn't get very far because reading about other people's dreams about flying, falling and having their teeth fall out proved far more interesting. There is a whole section about walking around naked or only wearing a Motel-Six-sized towel, a dream I've had several times, which apparently indicates feelings of vulnerability.

I had a similar nocturnal experience when my daughter had the lead in her school play in 8th grade. She was Scheherazade in "Arabian Nights" and I helped her with her lines one evening as we sat in the cool air on our front porch. That night I had the dream that I was in a play and didn't know my lines. This one is way worse than the exam dream. If you miss the exam, you will suffer some personal shame, but in a play, you'd be up there for an entire audience to experience your humiliation. Fortunately I woke up before being on the receiving end of ripe tomatoes being hurled onstage.

I did some searching on the Internet for dream interpretation and even took a quiz at quiz.ivillage.co.uk/uk_astrology/tests/dream.htm. There is a question about money and I realized I never dream about money. Ever. So I had to make up an answer for that one. Anyway, my score reveals "I feel strong, confident and in control ... feel secure with myself and ready to take on any future challenges." I attribute this positive result only to the fact that I don't dream about screaming at old cars, rarely encounter hostile animals or find myself in prison in my dreams.

Then I took the dream again just for fun, picking the most violent responses, only to be told that I was bursting with anger and aggression.

But summer is almost here, and with its approach, I hope for an end to these dreams, replacing them with those marvelous flying dreams. My destination is not clear, but there will be no textbooks, no exams, no stage fright and I will be fully and most elegantly clothed.

Adventures in Babysitting

A teen's thoughts on procreation

We've been attending a wonderful new church where I actually get something out of the sermon. I walk out with thoughts and ideas on how to live my life, rather than trudging out bearing a boatload of guilt and a desire to flee from church property as quickly as possible before being sucked down immediately into the bowels of hell.

This past week we heard a wonderful sermon from the wonderful pastor Andy Stanley about the causes of conflict. He remarked that it is amazing that anyone ever gets mad at his or her mother. "Here is a woman who risked her life to give birth to you, took care of you for years when you could do nothing for yourself. Then one day, she says, 'Would you please clean out the dishwasher' and you think, I hate her!" He continued, "We should get down on our knees every day and thank our mothers!"

Along about this time I was regretting my decision to let my children sleep in and not attend church. But then I quickly realized that I could use it to my advantage. I'd tell them that someone in the hills of North Dakota had uncovered an addendum to the commandment that said "Honor Thy Mother and Father." It said, "And do whatever thy mother shall request of thee, even if thou be betweenst levels on a new video game and it's something really icky like cleaning up dog poop in the backyard."

But I figured that twisting a preacher's words to my own evil purposes seemed a tad outside the spirit of the sermon. I could see God picking out a fresh thunderbolt just for me.

And I realize that expecting our kids to show appreciation for all we've done and sacrificed for them before they reach their 20s, or the Parental National Bank is cut off, whichever comes first, is about like expecting my dog Riley to sit up one day and say, "Hey, thanks for all the Gravy Train and the mailman chew toy."

My son has shown minor slivers of appreciation in the past. One night he came upstairs while I was in bed watching TV. He looked at me, then the TV and said, "I can't wait until I'm a grown-up and get to just lie around and watch TV every night."

"Yeah, but then you're resting and your kids come up and say, 'I need a dozen cookies for a party at school tomorrow and a costume of George Washington with a curly white wig. I don't have any clean underwear and I've already worn this pair for three days.'"

He said, "I know exactly what I'd say about that."

"What?" I asked.

"Go talk to your mother."

So maybe that wasn't exactly appreciation, but it was acknowledgement of who attends to all his needs, which is something, right? But perhaps I'm doing no favors for his future wife.

But he does express gratitude. He had informed me that he is especially grateful that he will never, ever be a mother. That, plus a few more revelations have come from his latest job. He started babysitting.

A few weeks ago he came home from one of his babysitting jobs. He said, "Mom, I don't understand something. I took care of these kids - took them to the park, fed them and watched them for a few hours - and I got paid a lot of money. But their parents do that 24 hours a day, and have to buy all their food and toys and clothes, and they don't get paid anything. Why would anyone do that?"

I thought for a minute how to respond. Should I tell him we were worried about what to do with any potential pesky disposable income, and figured having children would be the best way to insure that we never actually had any. That plan worked beautifully, by the way.

"Because we thought every day with you would be filled with joy and make our lives so much happier," I said in not an entirely unserious tone.

So no one is bowing down before me on a daily basis, or thanking me for doing the grocery shopping, laundry, cooking or carpooling. And I still get gripes about empty-ing the dishwasher. But I'm grateful he's seeing firsthand a fraction of what it means to be responsible for a child. So to paraphrase those MasterCard commercials:

Cost of having a baby: $6,000

Cost of Legos, army men
and video games: $2,387

Cost of raising a son to age 18: $164,483
Having your son appreciate
to the teeniest extent what it
took to get him to age 13:   Priceless

☺   True Tales

A friend was talking with her teenage son one day. "There are three things I want you to promise me you won't do in high school," she said. "Have sex, drink or do drugs."

"Mom, I promise I'll never do drugs," he said.

We were at a lake house with another family one year. While floating around in the lake, their youngest daughter was getting repeatedly dunked. She finally shot up onto the raft, yelling, "I've got a nose full of snot, and I'm not afraid to use it!"

A dean at my kids' school tells this story. When his son was in 4th grade he was coaching his basketball team, and although his son enjoyed it, he had not discovered the "joy of giving it your all." So the dean had a talk with him and told him how when he was in high school he was the sixth man, always the number one substitute but not a starter. So the summer before his senior year he worked really hard, got stronger and faster, then made the team.

After this inspirational talk, his son said, "Daddy, before you were a starter, what did you do during the game?" The dean said, "Well, I watched and cheered, but mostly I sat and kept the bench warm."

"That must have been nice," his son said.

Six

Family Awards

No Mom of the Year

"I'm the world's worst mother!" I've heard friends exclaim mournfully. Then they will relate some minor infraction, like cutting their child's sandwich in half diagonally when the child will only eat it if it is cut into two rectangles. I always tell them my philosophy is that if you get to the end of the day and no one is in the hospital, your house and its contents have suffered little permanent damage from child-inflicted destruction and you have enough brain cells left to put your pajamas on correctly, then you're doing a fantastic job. And on really bad days, who cares if you wear your leopard print flannel top with your purple gym shorts to bed.

So, in the spirit of helping parents feel better about their parenting skills, I am going to confess to some of the things I've done in my years as a parent. You can also consider this my official withdrawal from nomination for the "Mother of the Year" Award.

Sometimes I sneak a brownie at 6:45 a.m., or toss a few chocolate chips on my cereal. If my children ask me what I'm eating, I tell them it's zucchini.

The summer before my son started kindergarten, he

began sleeping in his clothes. At first I thought I should discourage such behavior, but when I realized it meant he'd wake up for school already dressed, I let him do it.

When my children were little, I'd tell them to go to bed and that I'd be in a minute to read a book. Sometimes, I secretly wished they would just fall asleep so I could avoid reading "Green Eggs and Ham" for the 1,887th time and watch "Melrose Place."

One day I got so annoyed at hearing constant complaints about everything, that I told them my new phrase was "So what," which I then responded to everything they said until they got so frustrated they left me alone.

I consider Rice Krispies treats an acceptable breakfast. People eat cereal for breakfast and put butter on their toast and marshmallows in hot chocolate, so what's the difference? Along the same line, I count Spaghettios with meatballs and a fruit roll-up as a balanced meal.

I tiptoed into my children's rooms when they were babies and held a mirror to their mouths to make sure they were still alive on more than one occasion.

If the tape on a disposable diaper didn't stick, I used small strips of duct tape to make it stay on so I didn't have to throw away the diaper. When the children were in the phase of taking off their diapers to experience the thrill of being nude, I took the duct tape and wound it around a few times (Of course, it took us about half an hour and an Exacto knife to get them out of the diaper.)

I didn't buy my children shoes with shoelaces until they begged me to because they were being mocked by their peers. I rank Velcro up there as one of man's greatest inventions and saw no reason to subsidize the shoelace industry.

When we go through the drive-through at Wendy's or

McDonald's and take the food home, I put most of the fries on their plates, but leave a few in the bags. Then I sneak the bags into another room and eat the rest of the fries.

My son wore my daughter's hand-me-down pajamas when he was a baby. That probably would have been fine, except they had "Daddy's Little Girl" written all over them.

If necessary, I have pulled a shirt off the top of the laundry pile, rubbed it with a fabric softener sheet and given it to a child, claiming, "Of course it's clean!"

Once, when my daughter was in preschool, she got an invitation to a birthday party from a child I'd never heard of, a child who lived far away and whose party ended at peak traffic time. I tossed the invitation and never told her.

In the days when I was teaching parenting courses, I once talked to a woman on the phone about the benefits of my particular course in "encouraging positive behavior" - while my son was tossing chocolate chip cookies across the room.

Sometimes, when one of the kids is talking to me and reciting the entire plot from another episode of "Rugrats" or telling me the same knock-knock joke for the 187th time (the one about the bananas and the oranges), I act like I'm listening, but I really think about whether that new jacket I bought will go with my black jeans, and whether it will look so stunning my co-workers won't notice that I wear the same outfit every Friday.

The worst thing I've ever done? I've forgotten the tooth fairy. Twice.

Awarding Myself

Mom wins dubious honors but no trophy

When the Olympics came to Atlanta, our family talked a lot about winning and medals and trying to do your best. My children pulled out their various sports trophies; small plastic gold statues probably worth about $1.87 retail, but are priceless to them.

"Mommy, did you ever get a trophy?" my daughter asked.

I thought hard. No, not one. I had never gotten one single trophy in my entire life. I'd had my share of academic honors, but somehow I knew my piece of laminated paper with Honors for Trigonometry just wasn't going to impress her. She was looking for that gleaming gold statue.

I'll admit, I didn't really excel at sports as a child. The most dreaded time of the school year for me was the Presidential Fitness Test. I dreaded that like a camper dreads a wedgie.

I wasn't a slug. I was always the first girl chosen for

softball games, and I did come in second place one year for jumping rope the most times, I don't even think I got a ribbon.

Trophies weren't awarded as freely in those days, before building self-esteem overtook the pursuit of knowledge as a school's primary focus.

So I decided to retroactively award myself some trophies for events at different stages of my life. Here are a few I could have won.

Last Girl in Elementary School to Go Steady. While all the other girls were wearing boys' ID bracelets, I was left to ponder the mysteries of attracting the opposite sex. Apparently, sporting crooked teeth, crooked pigtails; blue cat-eye glasses and wearing homemade dresses on my unpleasingly plump frame were not the way to go about it. In fourth grade, I had a major crush on a boy I'll call Todd. I used to stare at him when we had movies in science class about beavers building dams, and the lights were low.

One day after school, I was working on a project with two friends. We were making Mount Olympus out of papier-mache, complete with Barbie and Ken dolls dressed as Zeus and Athena in toilet paper togas. One friend revealed that Todd had asked her to go steady. I was so upset I caught my finger in the electric mixer we were using to mix up the papier-mache. It was my first, and one of my most painful lessons about love.

Girl In High School with the Most Unusual Writing Instrument. My dad used to keep a big wad of pens in his dresser drawer. When I couldn't find a pen, I'd go in and grab one. One day I found an orange pen with a plastic window on the side. I really liked the way it wrote so I took it to school.

During chemistry class, a classmate picked it up and examined it. She turned it around, looked through the plastic window and yelled, "You pervert!"

In the disruption that followed, I found out that if you held up the pen, looked through the plastic window and turned the top, you were treated to the sight of several scantily clad women. My dad claimed a woman in his office gave it to him. I was inclined to believe him because the same woman game him a mug with writing on it that looks Chinese. When you turn it upside down, however, it instructs you to do something to yourself that is very rude, not to mention physically impossible.

First Girl in College to Break a Bone. I had been at college five whole days when I attended a dance with my boyfriend. (Yes, I had learned how to attract boys. Carrying around the orange pen helped, not to mention losing the hairdo, the crooked teeth and the extra pounds.) Some people behind me, clearly under the influence of cheap college beer, fell, rolled into me and broke my right food. I was in a cast with crutches for eight weeks.

My parents begged me to come home, but they had not reckoned with the determination of an 18-year-old away from home for the first time. Who cared that my classes were miles away, that I couldn't even get my food by myself because it involved carrying trays, that I lived on the second floor of a dorm with no elevator, and that it rained constantly, the water threatening to disintegrate my cast. There were lots and lots of cute boys!

So I didn't have any trophies and those weren't even stories I thought I should share with my daughter, but at least I felt better.

I had achieved notoriety in some respects, pathetic and humiliating as some of the circumstances may have been.

Then I was reminded of a story a friend told me. She had a friend whose daughter asked her the same question about trophies. Her friends said, "Well, I did win a second place trophy for Best Cow at the State Fair one year." Her child said, "But mommy, you didn't win the trophy. The cow did."

Now that is depressing. There is livestock out there with more trophies than I have.

☺ From the Butsch House

One day my husband said he needed to get his tires rotated. Christopher said, "Don't they rotate by themselves?"

I was driving the kids around, as usual. I said something about "driving you kids all over creation!" Christopher looked up and around and said seriously, "Oh, is that what this area is called?"

Christopher and I were sitting by the fire looking at Riley, who was having a wonderful time playing with his lavender rubber cat-shaped toy. I said, "It must be fun to be a dog."

"I don't know," he said. "You don't get good medical care."

"We take him to the vet," I said. "What do you mean?"

"Well, when I throw up I get medicine and a hug. When he throws up, he gets thrown outside."

And The Winner Is ...

The Lee Awards

It's awards and beauty pageant season again - Golden Globes, Emmys, Oscars, Miss Universe. While I enjoy the guilty pleasure of watching the glamorous parade of movie stars with their evening wear, perfectly applied makeup and $300 hairdos, (and that's just the men) I decided I would like to see some awards real people could relate to.

The best way to ensure that my family would actually win one is to create them myself, which also guarantees that there would be no talent of any kind required and no swimsuit competition. (No way am I gluing spandex to my bottom and perpetuate the myth that women wear high heels with a bathing suit.)

So as I sit comfortably attired in my House of Gap designer wear, with absolutely no cleavage within a 37-yard radius, I proudly introduce the Lee Awards. These awards honor stellar achievements for everyday family life. They derive their name from a combination of "We bare-lee made it through another day. I can hard-lee believe you said that, and you narrow-lee escaped being tossed into the backyard with a Slim Jim for dinner."

That, plus Lee happens to be my middle name and I've never found any real use for it.

Most creative use of vegetables award: This award goes to the mother who was hosting a birthday party for rambunctious four-year-olds at her house. Having exhausted her supply of indoor games, and herself in the process, she gave them all a carrot and told them to go in the backyard and find the bunny. A good time was reportedly had by all, despite the fact there actually was no bunny in the backyard.

Any lengths not to hurt their feelings award: This award goes, hands down, to my mother. When my brother was a little tot he wanted to make a sandwich for her. He carefully assembled bologna, white bread, and a 1" layer of mayonnaise, which my mother dutifully ate. Except the "mayonnaise" was really recycled bacon grease my mother kept in the refrigerator in a mayonnaise jar.

They would have gotten extra credit if they'd only kept their mouths shut award: To the two little boys who were singing the Pokemon theme song, with the words, "You'll teach me and I'll teach you'" Their very impressed grandmother said, "That is so nice you are singing about God."

"It's not God, that's Pokemon!" they shouted.

The Let's Get Real award: This goes to my friend Sara, community volunteer, first grade teacher, mother of two, and possibly the busiest woman I know. She was hosting our group of high school friends around Christmas when the discussion turned to Teacher Gifts. She had received bath salts, which she promptly divvied up among us into Glad sandwich bags. "When would I ever have time to take a bath?" she asked.

The I'm only nine years old, but have already learned the ways of the world award: My son wins this for a conversation we had. "When I'm a grown-up," he said, "I'm going to go upstairs every night and lie in bed and watch TV from 9-11."

"Yeah, and you'll be lying there all relaxed and then your kid will come up and say, 'I need a Christopher Columbus costume by the morning, and the scout leader says you need to send two dozen cookies to the meeting tomorrow,'" I said.

"I know what I'll say then," he said. "You'll have to talk to your mother about that."

The worst investment in babysitting award: This award goes to the family who was having a big family gathering. Some of the adults offered the older children each a quarter to watch the younger children. Which they did. They watched them take a set of magic markers and draw all over the brand-new ivory-colored sofa.

He knows when you've been sleeping, he knows when you've been beating up your brother award for honesty: The winner of this award was a child at my son's school whose letter to Santa read "Well, I have been really mean to my brother this year so I probably don't deserve anything. That's your decision. But if you decide to bring me something, here is my address."

The truth hurts award: This award goes to my friend Larke's son, Walker. He was going to get a haircut and told his father, "I'll get mine cut just like yours, daddy. None on top."

The Queen of Denial award: Hands down, this award goes to my friend Nancy's mother. For years, Nancy's older sister had an imaginary boyfriend. He would send her presents and flowers at Nancy's house when her sister came for a visit. After the truth was known, Nancy's mother said, "I don't care if her boyfriend is imaginary. He's been very good for her."

The two wrongs don't make a Wright award: I proudly present this award to my friend Melissa's brother. When he was in 3rd grade, Sky had to do a report on the Wright brothers. He promptly went to the encyclopedia and copied the information. There was a picture of the brothers, labeled to identify them. Sky did his whole report on Wilbur (Right) and Orville (Left).

The Hail Mary and thanks for the kids' meal award: My friend Wendy's daughter Emilia is learning the Hail Mary. One line is "Blessed art thou among women and blessed is the fruit of thy womb, Jesus." Emilia, with her hands solemnly clasped in prayer, reverently says "... blessed art thou among women and blessed is the food in my room, Jesus."

The wayward sheep award: This award goes to some friends of mine who we met for lunch after church one day. We were all sitting outside under an umbrella, waiting for my friend's husband to arrive with their son. He came, with his son's friend. But not his son. My friend pointed out that they were missing one of their three children, to which he said, "I thought you had him!" The husband drove back to church, and after a series of cell phone calls between the husband and wife, we were relieved to learn that the child was safely attending the Spanish mass. They returned a short time later, with the child inexplicably wearing half of a volleyball on his head. We could only surmise that the tradition of covering one's head for mass had been resurrected and that the boy had done his best to comply, even if it meant pilfering mutilated recreational equipment.

The you'll have all you can handle when you get older award: I present this to my sister-in-law Julie. When my niece Claire was three and still working on pronouncing those pesky consonants, she told her mother she wanted to go to Blockbuster and rent "Wady and the Cwamp," or "Pawent Cwap." Julie told her she'd had enough of both of those and certainly didn't want to watch movies about them.

The Isaac Newton award for achievements in scientific experimentation: My nephew Connor wins this one. During Easter he loved playing with plastic Easter eggs. One day he couldn't find the plastic eggs. Being the self-sufficient guy he is, he resolved this issue by simply taking eggs out of the refrigerator. As my sister-in-law went up the stairs to check on him, she was greeted by raw eggs dripping down the stairs. Followed the trail of shells and egg whites to the kitchen, she encountered the remaining raw egg carnage and a very upset little boy, distressed at the discovery that when flung into the air, the refrigerator eggs did not bounce like the pink, blue and yellow plastic ones.

The thanks for making me feel better about my substandard domestic skills award: I would like to give this award to my daughter. One time I was attempting to make spinach rolls for my book club. I was fussing about the fact that they didn't look good, and she said, "That's okay mommy, they will still taste good. It's like people, it doesn't matter what they look like."

In closing our awards, I would like to offer one final award, which pertains to parents everywhere. And that is:

Best parenting advice from a friend: When you're totally stressed out, follow the instructions on the aspirin bottle. "Take two. Keep away from children."

Acknowledgements

First, I have to thank Tom Butsch, the wonderful father of our two glorious children. Obviously, I couldn't have had them without him. He is an outstanding role model for them and always makes time for his children. As predicted, our daughter had him wrapped around her tiny baby finger from the second they were born, and my son followed suit three years later. They are lucky to have him for a dad.

I want to thank my dear late mother, Jean Richey, who shared her huge capacity for love, patience and kindness with me. I thank God my children were old enough to know their beloved "Mimi" before she died. Mom, you would be so proud of them. We miss you every day but you'll be forever in our thoughts.

Thanks to my dad for always being there. It's no secret where my sense of humor (and loud laugh) come from. Also, thanks for paying for all that fancy education that helped me learn to put words together. Thanks to Helen Bell for marrying my dad and making him so happy, and for being such a great cook!

I also want to thank Judy Bass, who was my college roommate and remains one of my best friends to this day. She provided encouragement and excellent proof-reading skills for this book.

I'd like to thank Lelia Kelly, my oldest friend in the world, whose bright spirit and writing talent are an inspiration. (She's written three legal thrillers – check them out at www.leliakelly.com).

Thanks to Peter Bowerman, author of "The Well-Fed Writer" who generously shared his knowledge of the publishing business with me.

Thanks to Jan Bilthouse, mom of two, who wrote me a letter saying that she was collecting all my newspaper columns in a book to give to her daughters. Thanks for the encouragement, Jan! It took me a few years, but here they are - in a book!

Thanks to my brothers and their families, Lynne Clyde and Greg Richey and Chris and Julie Richey for sharing their stories and for giving me my adorable nieces and nephew, Claire, Kate and Connor.

I wish to thank all the parents who contributed stories to this book, whether they knew it at the time or not, and whose little darlin's provided so many of the anecdotes. I especially wish to thank the members of my Bridge Club. Although in the 20 plus years we've been meeting, we've never once played bridge, we still manage to have a good time. And a great big thanks goes to the lovely ladies of my Book Club, with whom I've shared insights, stories, laughs, confessions and endless glasses of wine for the past 17 years.

Thanks to Stephanie Oswald, Tom Calk, George Long, Melissa Heath and Brian Zimmerman for saying nice things about the book for the back cover.

And lastly, thanks go to Chris Schroder, who let me start a parenting column in the pages of his newspapers and encouraged my writing and journalism career from the start. He spent countless hours with me in the production of this book - from proofreading to instructing me in the quirky ways of Quark to printing pages. This book would not have happened without his endless patience, guiding hand and never-flagging support.

He is also the love of my life and brand-new husband. (Don't tell him, but I think my next book is about all the wacky things that happened while planning our wedding.) I look forward to many more years of happiness with him.

I also with to thank the huge, wonderful, loving Schroder family, whose members have been so kind to me and so much fun to be with.

Thanks to every person who buys this book. If you can get just a few laughs out of it, and pass along a few hugs to your children, I've accomplished my goal.

If you have any stories you'd like to share or comments on the book, please e-mail me at jbutsch@mindspring.com. For updates on this book and upcoming ones, please visit schrodermedia.com or justastage.com.

Thanks for reading and happy parenting!

Jan and her two children, at ages 11 and 8.

About the Author

Jan Butsch is an native of Atlanta and a graduate of the University of Virginia.

After stints as a paralegal and manager at the High Museum of Art, she stayed home to raise her two children. She rejoined the work force as a writer for Schroder Publishing's newspapers, *Atlanta Intown* and *Atlanta Buckhead*, eventually becoming editor. Her parenting column for the newspapers won six finalist Green Eyeshade Awards from the Society of Professional Journalists.

Her work has appeared in *Elle* magazine, *Skirt!* magazine, *Atlanta Parent*, "Chicken Soup for the Expectant Mother's Soul" and *travelgirl* magazine, where she is managing editor.

Jan also writes a humor column and a restaurant column for *The Story* newspapers in Atlanta, where she lives with her husband and two children.

Jan Butsch
2114 McKinley Rd

Atlanta

30318

Tom Murphy

2990 West Roxboro Rd

Atl. Ga 30324